RECIPES FOR
SURFACES

VOLUME II

RECIPES FOR
SURFACES
VOLUME II

NEW AND EXCITING IDEAS FOR DECORATIVE PAINT FINISHES

Mindy Drucker and Nancy Rosen

A FIRESIDE BOOK
PUBLISHED BY SIMON & SCHUSTER

NEW YORK   LONDON   TORONTO
SYDNEY   TOKYO   SINGAPORE

To my parents, Shirley and Burton Drucker,
with love and gratitude
— M.D.

To my daughter, Vanessa, my most beautiful creation,
my most important accomplishment
—N.R.

Fireside
Simon & Schuster Inc.
Rockefeller Center
1230 Avenue of the Americas
New York, NY 10020

Text by Mindy Drucker and Nancy Rosen
Design by Jan Melchior
Photographs by Mark Seelen
Illustrations by Erik Sheets
Decoupage illustrations by Barbara Everard

A Packaged Goods Incorporated Book

Conceived and produced by
Packaged Goods Incorporated
9 Murray Street
New York, New York 10007
A Quarto Company

10 9 8 7 6 5 4 3 2 1

Drucker, Mindy
        Recipes for surfaces volume II: new and exciting ideas for decorative paint finishes /
Mindy Drucker and Nancy Rosen.
             p.   cm.
        "A comprehensive guide to more than 30 of today's techniques in home design—
with foolproof recipes for walls, floors, ceilings, doors, woodwork, and furniture."
        "A Fireside Book"
        ISBN 0-684-80179-5
        1. House painting. 2. Decoration and ornament. 3. Interior decoration.
I. Rosen, Nancy, 1057-   . II. Title
TT.323.D777   1995
898'.1—dc20   94-30575
                                                                        CIP

Color Separations by Wellmak Printing Press Limited
Printed in Hong Kong by Midas Printing Limited

ACKNOWLEDGMENTS

To my brothers-in-law, Mitchell Gold and Robert Williams, furniture makers whose designs and fabric choices, as well as insights into the way people live today, inspired my thinking. To the rest of my most patient and understanding family—Rhoda and Jack; Shirley and Burton; David, Alyssa, and Ilana; Chuck and Donna—always ready with a pep talk, devoted despite selfish (and lengthy) conversations about the creative process. And to the most patient and caring pair of all: my wonderful husband, Richard, who did his best and more to "keep the ship afloat"; and my darling daughter, Adrianne, an almost-three-year-old who never let me forget through the whole writing process that being "mommy" means most.

—M.D.

Special thanks to Melissa Merendino and Rob O'Connor. In addition to running their own contracting businesses, they make time to work and teach with me in my studio in Maplewood, New Jersey. To my lifelong friend Francine Rothschild, who introduced me to decorative painting along with a lot of other great things in life. Creativity grows best with experimentation, shared ideas and encouragement. I am lucky to be surrounded by people who have helped to make this all so much fun. Thanks Mr. Wilson, Love Dennis.

—N.R.

Nancy and Mindy would also like to extend special thanks to the following people and companies: interior designer Jeffrey Brooks, of Oldwick, NJ, for bringing writer and painter together; photographer Mark Seelen for working so diligently to present the recipes in the clearest possible light, as well as for being so wonderful to work with; Melissa Merendino, accomplished fine artist and decorative painter, of Norwalk, CT., for brainstorming and assisting with painting for the project; muralist Nick Devlin, of Tewksbury, NJ, and Jeffrey Brooks, for allowing us to include a fine example of decorative painting, the designer-showhouse room with which Nancy assisted them, in these pages; master painter Rob O'Connor, of Milburn, NJ, for his insights into painting interiors and furniture; Steve Marcketta, of Suburban Paint, Milburn, NJ, for his expert work on the paint formulas provided in this book; to Werner Meier of Design Impressions Gallery of Short Hills and Wall, NJ, for contributing fabric used in the book; Kevin Kelly of Structural Arts for his connections; Jan Melchior, for her great book design; Anne Newgarden for her careful copy editing; Marta Hallett, Kristen Schilo, Margaux King, and Tatiana Ginsberg of Packaged Goods Inc., for their help in bringing this book to life.

Packaged Goods Inc. would like to thank Dominic Berretto, Angie Hice, Jim Naughton, and Barry Silverman at Home Depot for their contribution of time, materials, and support. We also thank Allen Shefts at Pearl Paint/Pearl Art and Crafts stores for his generous donation to this project.

CONTENTS

FOREWORD
How to Use this Book

All the information you need to create more than 30 decorative paint finishes in the latest colors is right in your hands, in a format specially designed to make the process as easy as possible. Just think of this how-to guide as a cookbook, and the painted finishes as chef d'oeuvres that, with a little practice, are well within your creative grasp.

Decorative painting and cooking have a lot in common. Both have basic recipes and procedures—in cooking, how to prepare a pie crust, make a sauce, design a menu; in painting, how to prepare a surface, mix a glaze, plan a color scheme.

Like the first volume of *Recipes for Surfaces*, the new *Recipes for Surfaces Volume II* has been modeled after a good cookbook. At the heart of the book are the detailed "recipes" for creating each finish. These step-by-step guides show photos of each crucial step, as well as the finished effect and, where appropriate, the natural material that inspired the finish in the first place.

Each recipe is self-contained; you'll find a "recipe card" listing all the tools needed, what surfaces a finish particularly suits; how many people can most easily execute it; whether you must varnish the finish; and paint chips showing the colors of the finishes pictured. In addition, the introduction to each recipe discusses decorating styles it works well with, other tools you can use in creating it, additional color suggestions in which to execute it, tips for making the job simpler, and more.

Although geared to beginners, the book offers a range of recipes, identified by degree of difficulty on their recipe cards using paint-can symbols ( ). The simplest recipes feature one paint can; the most challenging, three paint cans.

Even the most challenging recipes are probably within your reach. To insure success, read the whole recipe before you begin, as well as the introduction to the chapter it is in. Also review the general information in Part One of the book on color, tools, paints, surface preparation, and more.

Then prepare samples. Test your colors and patterns on large pieces of illustration board, studying them in the light of the room in which the effects will be seen at several different times of day. (Colors change with the light: A pleasing blue in morning sunlight might turn dull gray at dusk.) See Chapter Five, *Before You Begin*, for more on making samples.

Some techniques, such as marbling, combine several skills, from simple sponging to free-hand painting. Don't be distressed if abstract versions are all you can master at first. In fact, this more casual style is often better suited to today's decorating styles. Of course, if you have your heart set on lifelike marble, you may want to hire a professional decorative painter and use the ideas in this book to convey to her the look you want.

One thing you won't find in this book are shots of elaborate interiors. This is done to help eliminate distractions and encourage you to study the techniques for themselves. It can be hard to focus on a finish in a room full of furnishings, flooring, and fabrics. And it can be hard to tell if a color in a photo of a room might suit your space because of the great variations in light that might exist between that room and yours.

For that same reason, most of the techniques in this book have been executed on pieces of sheetrock under the same lighting conditions. Once you learn the techniques, you can decide how best to adapt them to your particular spaces.

For those of you who have the first volume of this book, *Recipes for Surfaces*, please note that even a cursory comparison to *Recipes for Surfaces Volume II* will turn up numerous variations—the size of a cloth used to "rag" a surface, the kind of paint brush used to apply glaze, the way paint is mixed. As an eyewitness to the working methods of two different decorative painters who produced the finishes for these two books, I can report that both ways work extremely well.

What you'll find in *Recipes for Surfaces Volume II* are the exact paint colors, brush types, rag sizes, and everything else Nancy used to create the finishes shown here. But there is a clear and valuable lesson in the variations between the two books: You don't need to get hung up on the tyranny of only painting a certain way. You can substitute one tool for another. You can change the colors of a glaze. And you'll still get great results. In fact, you'll get a finish truly your own as well as a good understanding of how to execute the technique for future projects—all without the unnecessary angst involved in trying to create an exact replica.

What Nancy most wanted to share in *Recipes for Surfaces Volume II* is how easy and fun decorative painting can be—that, while steeped in tradition and technique, it also makes a simple, affordable, and attractive way to decorate your home today. To that end, everything in this book has been simplified as much as possible, often based on her experience teaching adult-education courses in decorative painting, so that you can get great results fast, with minimal fuss.

Look closely and you'll realize that many of the finishes you see in this book are the ones you see all the time in magazines and stores, often at hefty prices. The colors are from the latest decorating schemes, the ones projected by color experts to dominate in coming years. Go into any department store and you'll find sheet sets, lamp shades, picture frames, and even already-decorative-painted furnishings in the same colors as the finishes you see here. Using these "color suggestions," you can easily get a coordinated decorator look for your home. Or, if your walls are white and your furniture is inherited, you can use these finishes to update your interiors in the latest colors and "textured" looks.

Don't forget, however, that all this explaining on our part doesn't mean you can just dive right in. *You must practice before starting on your surfaces.* In fact, you'll see reminders to practice throughout the book. Take it from one relative novice to another: This is the key to success with decorative painting.

— Mindy Drucker

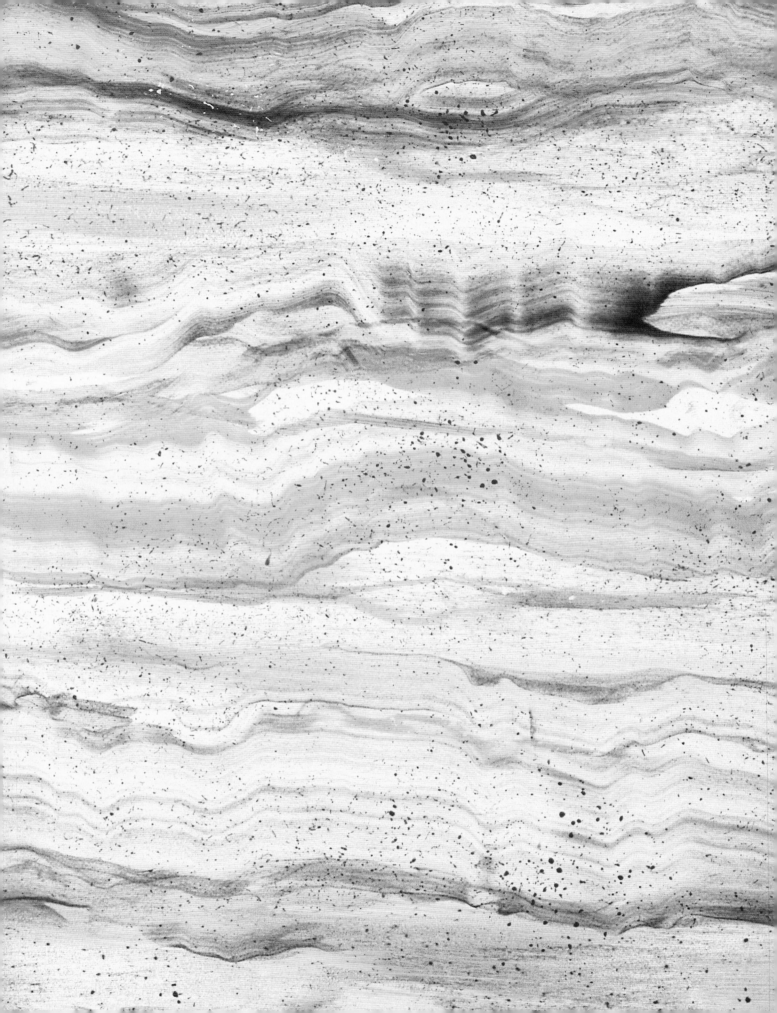

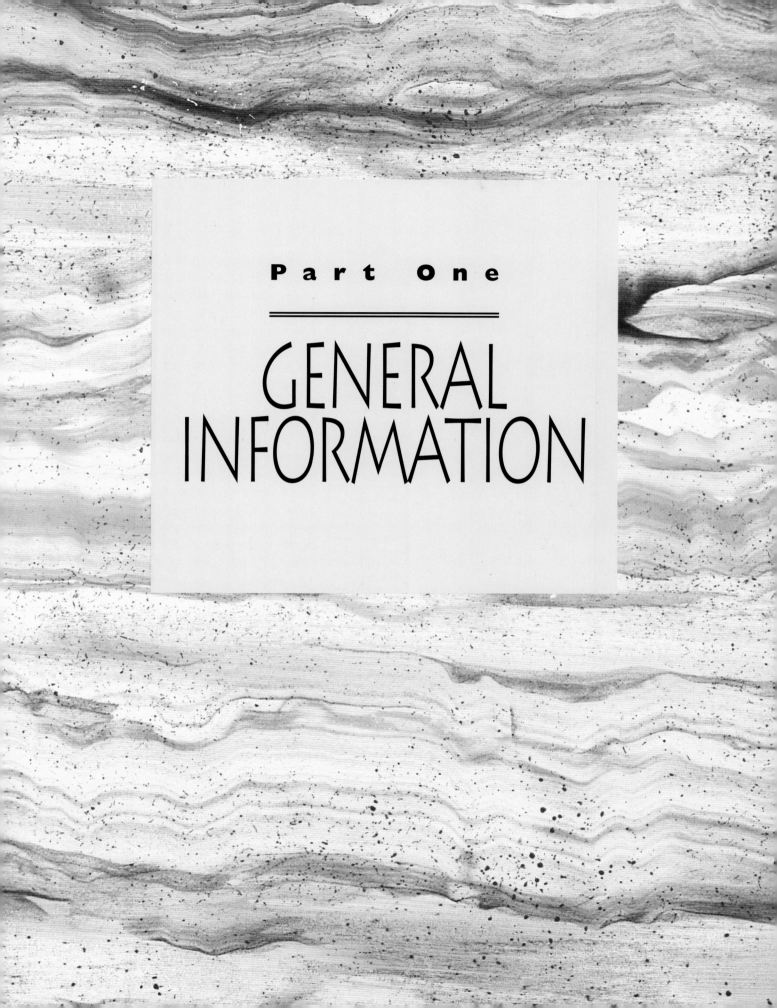

Part One

GENERAL INFORMATION

INTRODUCTION
WHAT DECORATIVE PAINTING CAN DO FOR YOU

A painted finish can serve many functions. Here, a "spattered" wall subtly introduces a host of colors, helps link the surfaces of the room, and makes a unique statement.

Decorative painting is everywhere you look these days, and its popularity is a real plus for do-it-yourselfers. How-to guides like this one have made "trade secrets" of this age-old art public. Paint, glaze, and art supply manufacturers have made the tools more widely available.

Along with a stronger presence on the interior design scene has come a looser, more casual approach to decorative painting. Classics such as marbling, graining, stenciling, sponging, ragging, and spattering still get a lot of play. But, as you'll see in this book, decorative painting also includes "printing" with tools as diverse as a feather duster or paint scraper.

Even the definition of decorative painting has been expanded. Traditionally, it means applying two layers of interior house paint (the base coat) and then topping them with a transparent paint layer called glaze. Because the glaze never fully covers the base coat, thus allowing some of the color beneath to show through, your eye does some mixing of its own right on the surface, creating a rich hue with a sense of depth.

In some cases, the process is even easier; instead of glaze, the top layer is simply opaque paint. Because of the way in which it is applied, the top paint layer still never fully covers the base coat, causing a similar mixing by the eye.

A host of reasons account for the recent popularity of decorative painting: its ability to serve as a more affordable stand-in for wallpaper; the way it can transform a flea market find into a treasure; the diversity of color it can create. But perhaps the biggest reason is the way it can coordinate with so many of the latest decorating trends. It is amazing and wonderful that you can transform your home, or just certain rooms, into brand new living spaces.

ADDING TEXTURE

A good example of this is how these finishes can add "texture" to a room—or, more accurately, the *impression* of texture. By applying glaze or paint with tools, from sponges to rags to combs, rollers, and brushes, you create flat patterns that the eye interprets as texture, a welcome addition to many looks.

Texture is central to a monochromatic color scheme. Picture the classic all-white interior. Where does the design interest come from? A subtle blend of tones and textures: off-white linen sheathing the walls, gauzy-white draperies at the windows, crisp-white canvas slipcovers on the furniture, warm-white crewelwork rug underfoot.

Texture is also in keeping with the trend toward eclecticism, mixing and matching materials within a room. For example, in a dining room, instead of a matched set, you might find a glass table ringed by upholstered chairs and paired with wood cabinetry. Surfaces in a decorative finish can hold their own in such a mix.

The same can be said of decorative painting with "global," or "ethnic," design styles; the "texture" of painted finishes can help balance strong elements in a room. In Chapter Ten, *"Textured" Wall Finishes*, you'll find several easily attainable decorative effects that would fit the bill.

INJECTING COLOR

Another way decorative painting fits today's styles is through color. Color is the heart of decorative painting. It is by picking the right colors that you'll be able to recreate many of the decorative-painting looks you see in stores and magazines today.

There are several ways to do this— and the easiest is right in your hands. Paint formulas for the colors used for the finishes are given in the back of the book. The colors here were developed with an eye toward reflecting the latest styles seen in decorating magazines, catalogs, and stores, and were chosen based on the latest research into the color trends most likely to prevail over the next five years and beyond.

Note, however, that the colors suggested here are meant only to give you an idea of what's "hot" and what's coming. You must combine this information with your personal taste, the furnishings you have and those you plan to buy, as well as where and how you live, to come up with the colors and styles of decorative painting that are right for you. The power of decorative painting lies in its easily attainable ability to make your decor unique. Don't be a slave to either fashion or "expert opinion." Nobody knows better than you what you'll be happy living with.

CONVEYING STYLES

As you'll find in Chapter One, color can perform many functions, from giving rooms a restful or lively ambience to making a space seem larger or cozier than its size.

Color can also help you express decorating styles. Following are four color palettes from which the colors in this book were selected. Loosely, they represent four very broad decorating styles or sensibilities with which you can imbue a room.

However, keep in mind that there is much cross-over among the color groups, and that color *combinations* are a major part of what makes an interior color scheme work. The neutral palette could easily accept accents from any of the other groups. A fresco-pastel might make the perfect glaze over a base coat in a deep jewel tone.

In addition, colors from each group are used in varying intensities and values—i.e., a modern bright toned down with gray or white. They have also been used in varying quantities, thus greatly altering their impact. To get a certain look, you won't use all the colors in a group at once; nor will you be using them in the same quantities within your space. That's why two strong colors that look like they'd never "match up" may work beautifully together when one is on the walls, the other is used as an accent, and there are soothing neutrals between them.

Using neutral hues in stenciling helps you couple natural colors with innovative designs.

NEUTRALS

The biggest color story is the move to a more natural color palette. Perhaps part of the rising tide of environmentalism, the new neutrals are more reminiscent of earth tones, going beyond beiges and grays into yellows and greens. Sophisticated and subdued, they are beautifully served through decorative painting's layered effect.

In decorative painting, these tones help you recreate natural materials such as leather, stucco, and stone. (See recipes, Chapters Seven and Nine.) They can be great backdrops for the fine wood furniture of Modern design as well as the wide-ranging collectibles of Country style.

They are also good foils for the trappings of "global" style, which can include a broad array of multicultural influences from our own country and the world marketplace beyond. They blend with the natural materials of the style—sisal, rattan, tortoiseshell, mahogany—and provide a framework for the strong patterns, often in the form of batik-like fabrics in rich hues, that are one of its hallmarks.

FRESCO-INSPIRED PASTELS

Pale violet, sage green, dusty rose—these soft, yet rich and warm, colors inspired by fresco painting are the new pastels. Toned down, they tie in well with neutrals to create finishes with complex coloring and great depth. These grayer, dustier pastels have a comfortable, casual, well-worn feel, like that of faded floral slipcovers or a favorite old cotton shirt.

You can match them comfortably with decors as diverse as Santa Fe and Victorian, the latter, incidentally, a period in which decorative painting flourished. They are also the colors of rich yet subtle Pompeii-inspired interiors. You can see decorative-painting examples of this color palette in the "Sedimentary Style Marble" finish, the "Fresco" finish, and the "Stenciled Tile" effect.

MODERN BRIGHTS

One important influence on color trends is technology. Today, manufacturers of many materials for the home, from fabrics to flooring, can use technology to more easily create brighter colors than ever before. This has brought new freedom in creating coordinated decorating schemes with modern brights, a palette of hues reprised from the 1950s.

Daring shades of lime and lemon, salmon, coral, and periwinkle can help create lively interiors with a contemporary air. Yet, they can be relaxed, too, bringing to mind the casual feel of island living. This versatility makes bright hues an exciting option.

Combinations of brights aren't as shocking as they might first seem. You find them together often in nature; because they work so well, you may not have stopped to think about it. They work because they have similar color intensity, a characteristic that creates a balance among them—no one strong hue dominates and draws the eye. (For more on color characteristics, see Chapter One, *Color: The Flavor in Every Recipe.*)

Many of these brights seem to have come straight out of an English country garden; they can often be found in the Laura Ashley-type floral prints typical of the English Cottage style. These days, even more than the hues of blooms, the color emphasis is on the greens of the garden's foliage.

A single bright teamed with white or a neutral can make a striking statement—in a room, or when combined in a decorative effect. See, for instance, the "Feather-Duster Finish," or the "Blue Marble" technique.

JEWEL TONES

These dark colors make strong statements in a room setting. They are the colors of the English hunting-lodge style as well as the traditional "library look." Jewel tones are also great accent colors—witness the strength of sapphire, ruby, and emerald Colonial glass pieces in a natural decor. They convey opulence and formality, tying together rooms filled with classic luxuries: gilt mirrors, velvet sofas, and tassled pillows.

Jewel tones draw the eye to the surface they adorn. Used simply they enhance, not overwhelm.

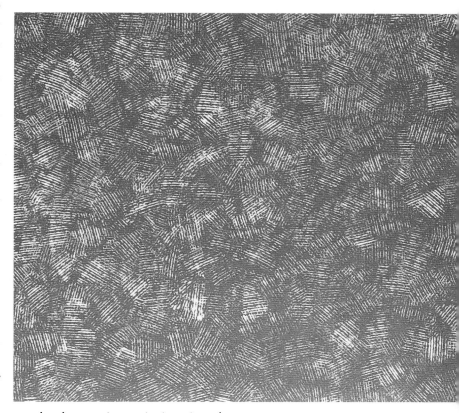

In decorative painting, jewel tones make great base-coat colors, seen peeking through a light-colored glaze—see, for example, the richly colored surface you can create with the "Corduroy Ragging On" technique. The jewel tones are also great complements to metallic finishes, such as those you'll find in Chapter Six, *Metals*.

CHAPTER ONE

COLOR:
THE FLAVOR IN
EVERY RECIPE

Sweet success with decorative painting comes from a mix of many ingredients, but none is more important than color. It's easy to see why. Color can transform the character of a finish, taking it from subtle to bold, traditional to contemporary, formal to casual.

In the introduction to this book, there are a host of ideas on how to use painted finishes with today's most popular decorating styles. The key to doing this is knowing which hues can help you capture the look and feel of a style.

That's how the colors for the finishes in this book were chosen—based on current design trends. In these pages, you can find the same looks you love in stores and magazines, and then use the color suggestions and guidance supplied to achieve these looks much more affordably.

Don't forget that you can also use the "mix-and-match" principle: Maybe a finish you like isn't shown in colors that suit your decor; but another finish is. You can take the formulas for the other finish to the paint store, and have its colors made up for you. Be sure, however, to follow "paint-system" and "paint-consistency" requirements for the recipe you'll execute. (For more on paint systems and consistency, see Chapter Two, *Paints and Tools*.)

There is, of course, no reason to limit yourself to colors pictured here. In fact, the best way to think of all the recipes is as "serving suggestions," much like the recipes you might find on a box of pasta. There are so many variations; we have only scratched the surface of the great array of colors and patterns decorative painting makes available to us.

Sometimes, so much choice can be a little unnerving. You're probably well acquainted with the challenge it can be just to pick standard paint colors for a room—coordinating with elements already in place, dealing with the pressure of knowing you'll have to live with your choice for some time. And even if you narrow your options to safe-and-neutral white, there are all the subtle shades that fall under that heading.

With decorative painting, it can be even more challenging. You must pick more than one color for each surface and make sure those colors work well together.

To better your odds of successful selection—whether you plan to buy your paint and glaze ready-mixed or mix them yourself—it pays to know something about color: the way colors work together, the interior design rules governing them, even how they influence the way you feel. The best place to begin is with a quick look at the concepts known as "color theory" and how they work in interior design.

UNDERSTANDING COLOR

When it comes to identifying pleasing color schemes, our earliest paint-box lessons still apply: Any hue can be made by combining the three primary colors— red, yellow, and blue—plus varying amounts of black and white. By mixing pairs of primaries, you form the three secondary colors: red and yellow make orange; yellow and blue make green; blue and red make violet. Then, by blending the secondaries, you get the tertiaries: olive, for one, which comes from mixing green with violet.

Today, however, thanks to technology, we should probably qualify the basic rule to say that *almost* any color can be created from the primaries. In reality, the more colors you combine, the less vibrant your result will be. So manufacturers now produce a wide range of colors whose brilliance would be hard to match by starting with the primaries.

COLOR HARMONY

To grasp the relationships among colors, you can use the color wheel, pictured here. Like the face of a clock, it has 12 parts. You'll find the primary colors at 12 o'clock (yellow), four o'clock (red), and eight o'clock (blue). The secondary colors are at two o'clock (orange), six o'clock (violet), and 10 o'clock (green). In the remaining six spaces are the intermediate colors, so called because they lie between the primary and secondary colors.

From the position of colors on the wheel, you can identify harmonious blends. Among recommended combinations are *similar* colors, such as orange and yellow, which appear near each other on the wheel. Other options are *complementary* colors, such as red and green, which appear opposite each other. Complementaries serve a special purpose in decorating: They tone each other down to help balance a scheme.

A color also blends well with the colors flanking its complementary—orange with either blue-green or blue-violet, for instance. This arrangement is called *split-complementary*.

You'll also discover that *triads*—any three colors equidistant on the wheel (the primaries, for example)—will harmonize.

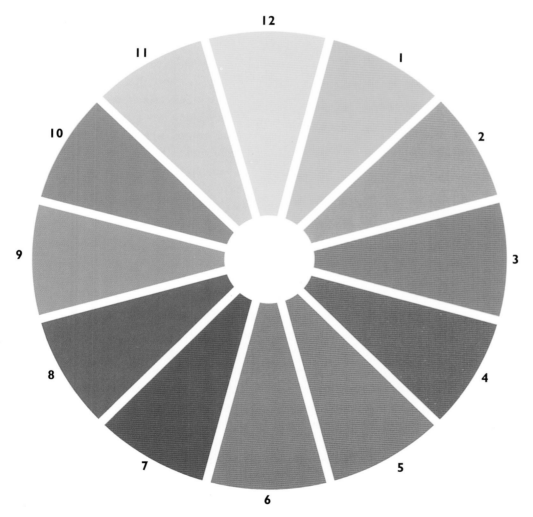

You can use a color wheel to get a feel for how colors work together. Keep in mind that colors on the wheel are in "pure" form; but the same principles apply to all their different values and intensities—i.e., pale pink would occupy the same space on the wheel as red.

COLOR CHARACTERISTICS

Even though the categories mentioned might be unfamiliar to you, you'll probably find many of your favorite combinations fit into them naturally. You may not recognize them at first, however, because on the color wheel they are in "pure" form, and this isn't often the form in which they are used in decorating, of course.

A color has three main characteristics: its *hue*, the color family to which it belongs; its *intensity*, how dull or vivid it is; and its *value*, how dark or light it is. By varying the intensity and value of pure color, we derive a multitude of others.

For example, by altering the value of pure red, we can get both rose and pink, which belong to the same color family and, thus, share the same position on the color wheel. To change the value of a color, you mix black and/or white into it. Mixing in white creates a *tint*; adding black gives a *shade*; blending in gray makes a *tone*.

CLASSIC COLOR SCHEMES

Based on these principles, we can devise color schemes that are pleasing and easily achieved. Using different values of the same color—cream, taupe, and deep brown, for instance—will give you a monochromatic arrangement. The scheme can be enhanced by decorative painting's two-tone effect. Try taupe walls sponge-painted over with cream glaze to subtly add design interest to a subdued setting. Sometimes, the simplest schemes provide a dramatic effect.

You can also create a harmonious setting with different colors that have the same value: three deep jewel tones, for example. The contrast between, say, a rich red, gold, and green brings vibrance to the scene, while the similarity in values ties them together and prevents one color from dominating and throwing the scheme off balance.

Because you may not be used to thinking of colors in terms of value, identifying different colors with the same value may take practice. To get a feel for values, imagine looking at a black-and-white photo of a room of your house. Or, better yet, take an actual black-and-white photo of it. In the photo, all the colors that have the same value will be the same shade of gray. By diminishing obvious differences in hues, you can more easily spot those of similar value. (You may also be able to get a sense of similar values by looking at a room and squinting your eyes.)

Keep in mind that simplicity can be trusted when it comes to color schemes. Consider using just a range of neutrals—whites, beiges, grays. A subtle scheme like that makes a fine showcase for intricate painted finishes that might look busy or take a back seat in a more intensely colored setting.

Another option is to link your favorite hue with white or a pale neutral. In fact, using your preferred color as an accent will produce a scheme that is notable for its flexibility. As styles or your tastes change, you can just switch the accent color to give your neutral scheme a new look. Choosing a light accent color that contrasts less with your pale neutral background is a great way to give your interior a calming, relaxed air. Remember, too, that some of the most pleasing color combinations—and, some of the most unexpected—occur in nature; so keep your eyes open for inspiration.

CREATING A COLOR SCHEME

Interior designers have many methods for developing color schemes. A simple and effective one is to select the drapery or upholstery fabric first, and then create a custom look by matching walls, floors, and furnishings in coordinating hues.

If you're going to be mixing your own paints, picking your fabric beforehand is a safer bet. You can undoubtedly create a hue to match your fabric, but you might not as easily find a fabric to go with a distinctive color you've specially blended. If you'll be using premixed paints based on formulas given for the recipes in this book, you'll probably be safe picking your paint color first. The colors chosen for the finishes here were specially devised to coordinate with many of today's most popular decorating styles and home furnishings available at retail.

When decorating based on a fabric, professionals often advise that the background color of a print fabric and the base coat of your walls be the same. Then you can "pull out" other hues in the fabric pattern for coordinated accents; for a more sophisticated effect, you might want to skip the hue that appears in largest quantities in the pattern and bring out other colors instead.

Another method is to select three colors you like and apply them in varying quantities. Make one color dominant. Use the second color about half as much, and include the third as an accent.

A third way is to base your color scheme on a favorite object—a painting, a piece of pottery, an antique chair, a kilim rug. Its colors don't have to be the main ones in your room. You can create a neutral backdrop, then use the colors in your object as an accent.

COLOR CAN CREATE MOODS

Don't underestimate the power of color to establish a tone for your interiors. After a long day at the office, want to come home to a cool, peaceful oasis? Color can arrange it. Live in a space that gets little light, but long for a bright, eye-opening spot to have breakfast? Color has what it takes to create that too.

Color can help you give your home a single all-over ambience, or let you change the look from room to room. For instance, you can use soft hues that create a relaxed look for private spaces like bedrooms, then turn to deeper, more formal colors for areas in which you entertain.

COLORS HAVE TEMPERATURE

Red and yellow aren't the only "warm" colors; nor are blue and green the only "cool" ones. There are "warm" and "cool" versions of all colors. It depends on what other hues a color contains. Green with more blue in it will seem "cooler" than a green with more yellow.

Often, "more" might be just a few drops of a cool or warm color. Nowhere can this be better seen than in the great variety of "white" paints. Cool whites have the slightest bluish or purplish cast, while warm whites might carry a tinge of pink, yellow, red, or orange.

These little differences in quantity can make a big difference in the way a color is perceived in a room. For instance, warm whites appear to advance, while cool whites seem to recede.

Many people seem to favor warm whites for their living spaces, but cool whites also have a place. While a warm white might be welcome in a room that gets little sun, a cool one can be appreciated in a space consumed with warmth.

COLOR TRANSFORMS SPACES

Besides imparting your personal stamp and establishing a mood, color can visually alter a room. Consider these questions for each room you plan to paint, to determine the kind of "color therapy" you need. *What size is the room?* Remember that painting a room a light color will make it seem larger; applying a dark hue will give it a cozy feel. *What do you want the focus of the room to be—walls, woodwork, flooring, furnishings?* Varying the intensity of colors—that is, combining light or vivid hues with dark or dull ones—lets you place the emphasis where you want it. *What is the room used for, and how often is it used?* A hallway, for example, might be better suited to an especially stimulating color scheme because you

Light colors. Whatever hue you choose, light tints of it will give you a soft look. This easy-to-live-with quality makes light colors favorites in decorating, especially when livened with accents in a brighter or darker hue.

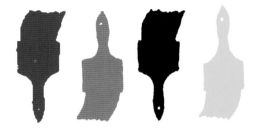

Bright colors. Even more exuberant than the warm colors, the brights include shades of blue, yellow, black, white, and red. They have a contemporary flavor. Except in children's rooms, we rarely see even two together. In groups, they can overwhelm.

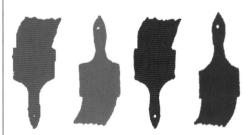

Dark colors. Black and other dark hues are less frequent choices for large areas of interiors. Jewel-tone colors, such as deep red, purple, green, and blue, have historical associations and a more formal air. These hues can be just right for the walls of a formal dining room or living room. But they more often serve as rich accents.

Dull colors. Shades of gray mellow the dull hues, which are said to help lower stress and bring on a contemplative mood. To keep them from seeming too vague, link them with bright accents. Experiment to discover the new options these hues can offer as part of a two-tone color scheme.

pass through it, rather than spend a lot of time there. *What are the color preferences of those who will use the room most?* For happiest results, review your choices with those who share the room. *Which direction does the room face?* A room that gets cooler north or east light might best be served by bright colors. *How much natural and artificial light does the room get?* Prepare paint samples of your colors and see how they look in the lighting conditions most common to the room. Examine how they look at different times of day. *Will spaces adjacent to the room also display painted finishes?* If you can see one room from another, you might link their color schemes by employing a common hue—the main color in one room could be an accent in the next, for example.

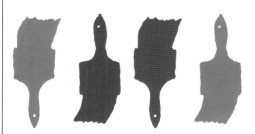

Cool colors. Cool hues, including blue, violet, gray, and green, give a feeling of calm. Perhaps their "coolness" stems from their association with water. This coolness has contributed to their popularity in hot climates. Be aware, that some cool colors contain red, and can appear warm.

Natural colors. Subtle and complex, natural hues can be soothing. In their simplicity, they provide a rich look. They can be pale, clear, dark, muted, or bright and are generally blends of many hues. To spice up dark or muted colors complement them with a bright hue also found in nature.

Warm colors. Ranging from red to yellow, these splashy hues demand attention, lend excitement, and "heat up" even a small, dark room. Psychologists speculate they may even increase our drive and help us work faster, making them a good choice for a kitchen or home office. Combined with cool colors, they always dominate.

Surprising colors. Rarely found in nature or teamed in daily life, they get our attention. Among them: hues contrary to their natural brightness—dull orange, for instance. Also: combinations with less contrast, such as magenta and purple. Note: colors in this category that once seemed startling have become conventional with frequent use.

CHAPTER TWO

PAINTS AND
TOOLS:
THE STAPLES

Before you head out to the paint store, you have a decision to make: Will you use water- or oil-based paints? Just about all paints comprise three elements: *pigment*, powder ground from natural or synthetic materials that give paint its color; *binder*, the vehicle that carries and fixes pigment and then dries to a protective film; and *diluent*, the solvents or thinners that dilute paint to a workable consistency. The differences between water- and oil-based paints lie in their binders and diluents. For water-based paints, such as latex or acrylic, the binder is acrylic resin, and the diluent is water. For oil-based, or alkyd, paints, the binder is usually linseed oil, and the diluent is mineral spirits.

PAINTS

BASE YOUR WATER/OIL
DECISION ON THESE FACTORS:

The finish you plan to execute. For a guiding hand in this area, turn to the recipe card in Part Two of this book for the finish you've selected to see which type of paint is recommended.

The surface you will paint on. Planning to paint the walls of your brand-new home? Set to spruce up some second-hand painted furniture? Or looking to rejuvenate a rusty old garden gate? See the chart at the end of Chapter Three, *Preparing to Paint*, for advice on the type of paint that will work best for your particular surface.

Also consider the pros and cons of each paint type:

OIL-BASED PAINTS

The Pros

- traditional medium for decorative painting that is particularly suited to advanced techniques such as wood graining
- a boon to the novice painter, especially in executing a more challenging finish, because oils dry slower and, thus, allow more time to work and fix mistakes
- dries to an especially durable finish that is well suited to areas that see heavy traffic or objects that get a lot of that "human touch"—like a hallway floor, or kitchen chairs, or baseboard and wall moldings that you might find yourself banging into with a vacuum cleaner on a regular basis

The Cons

- slower drying time means the project will take longer because you have to wait longer before recoating a surface
- cleanup takes longer than with water-based paints, and less-environmentally safe solvents need to be used
- safety precautions need to be taken because oils give off fumes and are flammable

WATER-BASED PAINTS

The Pros

- faster drying time—a plus when you need to apply several layers because you wait less time between coats
- easier cleanup—just requires water
- safer for you—they don't give off fumes
- safer for the environment—they thin with water and don't contain solvents

The Cons

- faster drying time— a problem when you're first learning a technique and need extra time to get it right; if you're working on a very large surface; or if you're trying to execute a "subtractive" technique (see Chapter Five, *Before You Begin*), generally considered a "two-person" job, with just one person. Suggestions for slowing drying times appear later in this chapter; but, depending on the technique, they may not be enough to allow successful execution in water-based paints.

Also note that although water-based paints like latex and acrylic are easily cleaned up when wet, they are permanent and water-resistant once dry. Drips and splashes are hard to wipe up. Remove them with denatured alcohol.

Choosing a Paint System

Remember that you're not just selecting the kind of paint for your finish coat—you're selecting a paint system. For a strong, durable finish, your best bet is usually to use the same paint type throughout your project—from primer to base coat to glaze.

This is especially true if you're using an oil system. A water-based acrylic glaze won't "take" over an alkyd base coat; the glaze tends to bead up and can chip and crack. (This is actually the basis for the "Crackle Glaze" recipe in Chapter Eleven).

There is one big exception to the paint-system rule that many people will appreciate: *You can paint oil over latex.* If your home is under 25 years old, your painted walls are most likely latex. Thus, if those walls have a good non-porous latex base in an appropriate color (paint must be satin, semigloss, or gloss to be nonporous), and you want to do a finish best executed in oils over them, go ahead. (Just prepare the walls as explained in the chart in Chapter Three.) Or, if you want to change the base color, you can still recoat with latex even if you plan to do your decorative finish in oils. The reason this is possible is that water-based paints dry quickly and fully, creating a surface that won't repel oil.

If your walls do have an alkyd base coat, and you want to repaint them with latex, you will need to apply a special primer first; see your paint or home store for recommendations. To learn more about the compatibility of base coats and primers, see Chapter Three, *Preparing to Paint.* See the following sections for the kinds of paints to buy.

WATER SYSTEM

BASE COAT

Buy latex interior house paint for your base coat. Latex interior house paint is the base coat for all the finishes in this book, whether the glaze layer uses water-based paint or oil. Benjamin Moore & Co. was used to create the *Recipe Paint Formulas* that are listed on pages 182-184. If you want to get the exact color of a base coat used in this book, you can either use the same brand or have the person at the paint store who mixes your base coat aware that she may need to compensate for any differences among paint brands.

Latex comes in several finishes: flat, eggshell, satin, and semi-gloss. For most of the finishes in *Recipes for Surfaces Volume II,* the base coat is semi-gloss.

In some cases, your choice will depend on the character of the finish. For example, anything that adds more sheen to faux marble might be welcome; but a faux-flagstone wall might look a little more natural with a flat or eggshell base.

Note, however, that if you are using a "subtractive" technique, in which you apply and then remove glaze or paint, you may be best off with a satin or semi-gloss base coat because they are less absorbent. To choose your base coat color, see Chapter Four, *Mixing Paints.* For the correct primer, see Chapter Three, *Preparing to Paint.*

GLAZE

Water-based glaze is mainly water (60 to 80 percent), which you combine with color in the form of water-based paints and acrylic medium, a transparent gel available in art stores and craft shops. Acrylic medium comes in matte, satin, and gloss finishes. Water-based glazes in a limited selection of colors are also available pre-mixed in art stores, home centers, and by mail.

In this book, with the exception of a special premixed crackle glaze in one recipe, no actual *water-based* glazes were used—a glaze being defined by its transparent quality derived from a glazing medium. The top coats on the water-based finishes are latex or acrylic paint, either straight from the can or diluted with varying amounts of water. On the recipe cards for those finishes, instead of a "Glaze" color, you'll find an "Applied Finish" color. (The oil-based finish coats, on the other hand, are for the most part actual transparent "glazes," made with oil-based glazing liquid.)

A closeup of a wooden chair reveals its "aged" finish. The effect was simple to achieve with the help of a special premixed crackle-glazing product.

This way of doing things contributes to the ease with which many of the finishes in this book can be accomplished. It also greatly shortens set-up time, eliminating glaze-mixing steps. Using paints instead of glazes does move the finished effects away from the transparency of traditional decorative painting. But, as the photos show, it can produce beautiful results all its own. You still get "depth" and softness by applying just a little bit of paint lightly in layers and by using tools whose "broken" impressions let the previous layers show through.

For thinning water-based paints and for cleaning brushes, use water. To find-out how to get the glaze color you want turn to Chapter Four, *Mixing Paints.*

OIL SYSTEM

BASE COAT

Today's oil-based interior house paints are alkyd paints, which are composed of a mix of oil and resin that dries faster and contains no lead. Alkyd paint comes in flat, eggshell, satin, semigloss, and gloss finishes. Satin is often recommended as a base coat for decorative painting. Alkyd is best thinned with paint thinner.

To find out how to get a base-coat color, see Chapter Four, *Mixing Paints.* For the correct primer to use, see Chapter Three, *Preparing to Paint.*

GLAZE

Transparent oil glaze is available premixed in cans from art and craft shops, as well as in some home centers and paint stores and by mail. To the glazing liquid, you will add color, usually in the form of universal tints, japan colors, artist's oils, or alkyd enamel paints. Liquid universal tints, often used by professionals, are concentrated and thus often the least expensive option when coloring large quantities of glaze. They come in easy-to-control squeeze bottles. However, they come in a smaller range of colors than artist's oils and, because they contain no drying agent, you shouldn't use more than 10 percent in your mix.

Japan colors are also concentrated; they produce flat color and dry fast. Available in cans, they may be hard to find. Sign painters use them; check paint stores, art supply stores, and craft shops.

Most of the oil-based glazes in this book use alkyd enamel paint, in a ratio of 20 percent paint to 80 percent glazing liquid—thus, when stocking up for your projects, you'll need to get much more glazing liquid than paint. Then you will probably need to add a solvent such as paint thinner (up to 20 percent of the total mixture) to get it to a workable consistency. But test before you start adding, and frequently as you add it in; too much will make the glaze run. See Chapter Four, *Mixing Paints*, for instructions.

Keep in mind that the proportions of paint to glazing liquid to solvent vary depending on the technique. For some, an especially watery and transparent glaze is desired; for others, a thicker consistency is a must. Glaze proportions may also differ from the proportions given in this book for a particular technique because of variations in the brand of glazing liquid you get versus the brands used in this book.

Read the label on your glazing liquid (and on all paint products). Reading the label with the "Flagstone" recipe was crucial because the glaze was to be used on a floor, and the label indicated the glazing liquid was suitable for that purpose. (Some glazing liquids are, while others aren't.)

Glaze and paint labels also give you a host of important information: how much glaze or paint to buy for a project (usually in the form of how many square feet you can cover with one can); how long paint or glaze takes to dry; and what kinds of safety precautions to take.

Making your own glaze. If you can't find ready-mixed oil glaze and you're at home "baking from scratch," you can make your own glaze with ingredients found in most art supply stores or mail-order art supply catalogs. The glaze, however, will dry slower and smell stronger.

To make the glaze, mix three parts turpentine to one part boiled linseed oil. (Linseed oil comes either boiled or raw; boiled is thicker and dries faster.) Then add a few drops of cobalt dryer or japan dryer, and color your glaze with paint or tints, as described above.

Premixed colored glazes. Note that you can also sometimes get a limited selection of premixed colored glazes. These, of course, will be much more expensive, and you won't have much control over color. But they might be a good (i.e., quick and easy) way of "getting your feet wet" on practice boards or a small object. Also, they may be easier to come by if you live in an out-of-the-way place. More and more, they are becoming readily available—we recently spotted a few in two home-furnishings catalogs.

Salvaging old glaze. When glaze gets old, a skin forms on top of it. Remove the skin by straining the glaze through cheesecloth or a disposable sieve.

The leopard skin effect, achieved via flogging.

METALLIC PAINT

Don't pass metallic finishes by because you assume they will be expensive and take forever to get the hang of. As Chapter Six of this book shows, those hot new-yet-old metallic finishes you see in all the stores on picture frames and lots of other accessories are accessible and affordable. Imagine the glow they can add to a room or a piece of furniture—say, for instance, enlivening the wooden legs and trim on a sofa.

The traditional decorative painting technique of gilding does require costly materials such as gold leaf and takes special skill to apply. There are books that detail this advanced technique, but training and experience are crucial to good results.

Instead, you can get the look with gold paint. There are several types, none of which actually contain gold. One type combines bronze powder and lacquer-based medium. Applying the paint over an ocher-colored base coat can help you achieve a truer "gold."

The simplest route to take is to buy metallic paint premixed. But you can also buy the powder and medium separately and mix your own. Note that the more powder you put in the mix, the more opaque the paint.

VARNISH

Varnish is a final transparent layer that protects your decorative finish and makes it last longer. It also determines the sheen of your finish.

To varnish or not to varnish? Good question. Often, it's optional. Many finishes are sturdy enough without it, and many surfaces (ceilings, most walls) don't get enough traffic or handling to require it. From some finishes, such as bronze or copper verdigris, varnish would actually detract, its sheen (even a low-luster one) looking out of place on a piece you've carefully "aged." And on a less-than-perfect wall that you've tried to camouflage with a flat, "textured" finish, varnish will give it a sheen that will underscore every defect.

On the other hand, as a shine-and-depth enhancer, it can only benefit certain finishes, no matter where you put them—marble, for example, as well as malachite, granite, and tile.

As a protector, it is indispensable for any faux-finished floor, tabletop, piece of furniture, cabinet, door, baseboard molding, chair rail, or other hard-use area. Delicate decoupage, whatever its locale, wouldn't be complete without several coats. And any finishes in "high-risk"

The rain-streaked appearance of weathered metal like this can be replicated through the "aged-metal" techniques in Chapter Six.

areas, such as hallways or children's rooms, deserve a few coats just to insure that your artistic endeavors aren't for naught.

To prevent your painted finishes from cracking, apply varnish only to surfaces that have fully dried (see "Drying Times," page 33). The varnish coats in this book were applied with an extra-large paint pad. See page 95 for a photo and instructions on applying varnish this way.

You can also roll varnish on or paint it on with special varnishing brushes made to hold large quantities of varnish. Keep these brushes just for varnishing. They are hard to clean, and if you leave even a bit of paint in them, the next time you use them for varnishing, the old paint might come out. In addition, they hold too much paint for regular jobs.

Like paint, varnish is best applied in several thin coats. Sand lightly between coats with 600- or 800-grade wet sandpaper.

Also like paint, varnish comes in both alkyd and water base. There are many kinds, some of which are available in a full range of finishes—matte, eggshell, satin, semi-gloss, gloss, and high-gloss.

One drawback of varnish: It tends to yellow over time, especially in a room that gets little sunlight. And the more coats of varnish you apply, the more it can yellow. In addition, some of the varnishes that yellow the most are the ones that provide the greatest protection.

This is especially a problem if the colors of your finish are light and the finish is in a hard-use area. For some projects, you may have to strike a balance between appearance and protection. Especially if you are using white latex paint, or any oil-based paint colors that you will be applying a water-based varnish over, test the effect on samples to get an idea of the amount of yellowing. (It's a safer bet to leave your finish unprotected for a few weeks than to varnish with the wrong product.)

Some kinds of varnish, and even some brands within each kind, yellow much less than others and thus would be your best choice for delicately hued work. A list of varnish types often used for interiors is included here; it indicates the general degree of yellowing each type is known to produce. In general, water-based varnishes yellow less. Some brands of varnish say "non-yellowing" on the label, but this may not really be the case, especially over white paint.

Which varnish to use will depend on your surface and your finish.

Note, however, that varnish manufacturers are currently addressing the yellowing and durability quandary. Ask your paint dealer for further recommendations.

Oil varnish. This varnish can be used over oil- or water-based paints as long as the finish is completely dry. Thin oil varnish with paint thinner. It dries to the touch in about three hours and dries completely in 12 to 24 hours. The higher the gloss, the more oil in it and the slower it dries. Oil varnish, especially marine varnish, yellows. Avoid using it over light colors.

Polyurethane. This works well over all oil- and water-based paints with the exception of artist's oils. It is especially good over free-hand painting, such as the veining in marble, which might peel if left unprotected. Thin polyurethane with paint thinner. Polyurethane yellows less than some varnishes, but it is not the best choice over pale shades. Wait at least 12 hours between coats.

Acrylic Varnish. Compatible only with water-based paints, it is acrylic medium (used for water-based glazes) thinned with water. It dries fast and is best rolled on so that it doesn't leave marks. It is odorless and yellows only slightly.

Water Polyurethane. Stronger than acrylic varnish, water polyurethane takes longer to dry. Thin it with water, if needed. Yellowing is minimal.

Polyurethane Gel Varnish. Made for furniture, this is polyurethane in a gel state that you simply rub on over a completely dry finish with a cotton rag or foam pad, applying it in the direction of the wood grain.

White Refined Beeswax. Rub beeswax on the surface with a cotton or linen cloth. Let it set; then buff it with a clean cloth. This clear finish doesn't turn yellow. If it gets dirty, you can remove it without disturbing the paint below. It must, however, be reapplied often, as needed.

How Much Paint?

Always buy or mix more than enough paint for base coats and glazes. Don't skimp here. Running out of paint in the middle of a wall will probably mean redoing the whole thing; the change in color with a new batch may be noticeable, and a dark line will show where you left off. Besides, you'll need extra paint for touch-ups down the line. And you may want to include the same paint colors in other rooms at a later date to create a coordinated look for your home.

First determine the square footage of your project. Then, to estimate the amount of paint you will need for your two base coats, read the label on the paint can to see how many square feet a can covers. Generally, a gallon of paint will cover about 300 square feet when applied with a roller or brush. A quart of

paint covers about 75 square feet. To be safe, however, subtract about 20 percent from the estimate given on the can.

For glaze, figure on about half the amount of paint you used for the base coat. (If you're having a house painter apply the base coats, ask him or her how much paint was used.) The glaze is usually a single coat and requires a thinner application; so you should have some left over for touch-ups.

Drying Times

Take drying times seriously—the success of your project will often depend on them. This is especially true for oil, but even latex paints don't dry immediately.

Keep in mind that there are two kinds of dry: dry to the touch and dry to the core, or cured. Paint dries from the top down; even if it feels dry on the surface, it might still be wet underneath. One layer must be cured before you add another. If a layer hasn't cured, and you recoat it, the second layer might bubble, peel, or crack. Or, especially when actively distressing a glaze, as in rag-rolling, you might break through the base coat beneath, destroying your finish.

Estimating drying times is difficult because many factors come into play. Paint dries by oxidation: When combined with air and light, it is transformed from a liquid into a solid. So, the amount of light and the type of weather are important; paint won't dry as fast in the dark or in a humid atmosphere. The sheen of the paint also counts: Flat paint dries more quickly than satin or semi-gloss. How absorbent your surface is and how thickly you apply the paint also matter. If acrylic paint is thinned with water, it dries faster. If alkyd paint is colored with artists's oils, it dries more slowly.

Here are some averages to give you an idea how much time to set aside for your projects. An alkyd base coat dries to the touch in three to four hours, but is best left overnight before recoating—and even then it is not fully cured. A latex base coat, depending on its sheen, takes about 20 minutes to dry to the touch and about two hours to be fully cured.

To speed drying of either oil- or water-based paint, use a fan in the room. For a sample or other small surface, use a blow dryer.

To slow drying time of an oil base coat or glaze, add a little linseed oil; but note that the more oil you add, the glossier the finish will be. To speed drying time, add japan dryer or cobalt dryer, available in art supply stores—but don't make it more than 5 percent of the total mix or the paint might crack.

With water-based glaze or paint, slowing drying time is a challenge. A good technique is to wet down the walls with a sponge before you start painting. Working on a humid day or turning on a humidifier will make the glaze stay wet longer, as will blocking out direct sunlight. You can also add a bit more water to glaze or paint, but be careful that it doesn't run. And you might try adding an acrylic gel retarder, available in art supply stores, to water-based glaze; but be sure it comprises less than 10 percent of the total glaze solution or it will weaken the paint.

The mask at left filters out dust and particles. The mask at right keeps out fumes.

TOOLS

A big part of the fun of decorative painting are all the tools you get to use. As in cooking, the more involved you get, the more paraphernalia you'll acquire.

A glance at the photo at the end of this chapter will give you an idea of the diversity of materials used to create the finishes in this book. Some of them you may already have, either in daily use or stowed in the basement, the remains of previous house-painting projects.

One option you'll see Nancy taking advantage of, particularly when working with oil-based paints: using disposable tools such as foam brushes, roller covers, and paint trays. If you only plan to do a few decorative painting projects, or you don't have the time and commitment to the cleanup required when using quality painting tools, you may want to try this option. You may also want to take this route if you are sensitive to solvents because it will lessen the time you are exposed to them. (Environment-wise, it may be a wash; you don't need solvents for cleanup, but you add to the trash heap with throw-away tools.)

For convenience and cost-savings, you can also use everyday items instead of "official" painting paraphernalia.

Paper plates can easily serve as painter's palettes. Plastic containers with lids can be reused as storage containers for paint and glaze.

To apply glaze in "additive" techniques or "distress" (remove) glaze for "subtractive" techniques, you'll use tools ranging from large feathers, a feather duster, and a paint scraper to sea sponges, paint brushes, and wide-wale corduroy. Once you're familiar with the basics of decorative painting, you may want to start checking around for items to use as tools to create your own unique finishes.

Safety Measures

- Make sure your work area is well ventilated.

- When opening a can of paint, wear goggles to prevent paint from splashing in your eyes.

- When sanding, or vacuuming up your work area after sanding, wear a mask designed to keep you from breathing in particles and dust. When working with oil- or alcohol-based products, using thinners, or spraying paint, especially if you are particularly sensitive to their vapors, wear a more elaborate mask designed with a special filter to guard against fumes. The masks come in different sizes; get the right size for you so that it gives a good seal. (See photo, page 33.)

- Wear latex gloves to protect your hands against solvents. Surgical gloves are recommended. They usually come in small and large sizes; for dexterity, get the correct size for your hands.

- Keep a bucket of water and perhaps a fire extinguisher nearby when working with turpentine, shellac, and other flammable substances.

- Don't throw wet rags soaked in oil and thinner in the garbage. Spread them out to dry outside or in a well-ventilated room.

For some techniques, specialized, sometimes-expensive paint brushes are traditionally used. Whenever possible, you'll find alternate suggestions of tools you can use instead right in the recipe.

Decorative painting tools also include items needed for preparation, paint mixing, and cleanup. Preparation tools for painting a room include:

Drop cloths or plastic sheets to cover furniture and newspaper to protect floor; lightweight stepladder in good condition and scaffolding for large projects and ceilings; soft, absorbent all-cotton rags for cleanup; sandpaper (in several grades) and a sanding block; tack cloth; vacuum cleaner or broom and dustpan; flexible compounding knife and spackling compound; steel ruler, metal straightedge, level, chalkline, chalk pencil or regular pencil, craft knife, and masking tape for measuring out designs; light-tack masking tape for covering areas you don't want to get paint on; paint roller, roller cover, and paint tray for priming and base-coating large surfaces.

Note that the nap of the roller cover should be suited to the job: For example, short nap is generally for smooth surfaces. Medium nap usually works well on most surfaces, but check with your local paint store for suggestions.

For paint and glaze mixing, you'll need paint stirrers (old long-handled round brushes can work well), plastic containers or paper bowls for mixing paint, and cardboard and white paper for testing imprints and painting samples. For cleanup, have on hand extra all-cotton rags, either water or paint thinner (depending on your paint type), plastic containers with lids for storing small amounts of leftover paints and glazes, and a laundry pen or stick-on labels to mark the contents on each container.

Brushes

Many of the painting tools that you will be using will be brushes. As with all painting tools, you will find it easiest when you use the right type, size, and quality of brush for each job. In fact, in decorative painting, the brush can sometimes determine the success of a technique.

An example is the decorative painting technique called "stippling," in which you dab a brush over and over against a surface, covering the surface with fine dots. A large stippling brush, which looks something like a scrub brush, can be quite expensive. No other tool, however, gives as soft and subtle an effect.

Good-quality brushes are hand-crafted from various materials. In general, synthetic brushes (often with bristles of nylon) are for water-based paints, while natural-hair brushes are for oil paints. (One reason is because strong solvents can damage a nylon brush.)

Natural-hair brushes are more expensive. Some types, from least to most costly, are pig, ox, squirrel, horse, and sable hair.

Gear the size of your brush to the job. To speed priming and base-coating of large, flat areas, you can use a roller.

If you use a brush, get the widest one possible (but not so wide that it overlaps the surface), and make sure you feel comfortable with it.

Brushes come in several shapes. For priming and base-coating large surfaces, you'll want a straight-edged brush; for trim, a chisel-edged brush. To smooth a glaze that has just been applied, professionals often use an oval sash.

Look for quality when choosing brushes. A good brush is thick and has bristles of various lengths, which allow it to hold more paint. The bristles should be springy, not stiff.

Decorative Painting

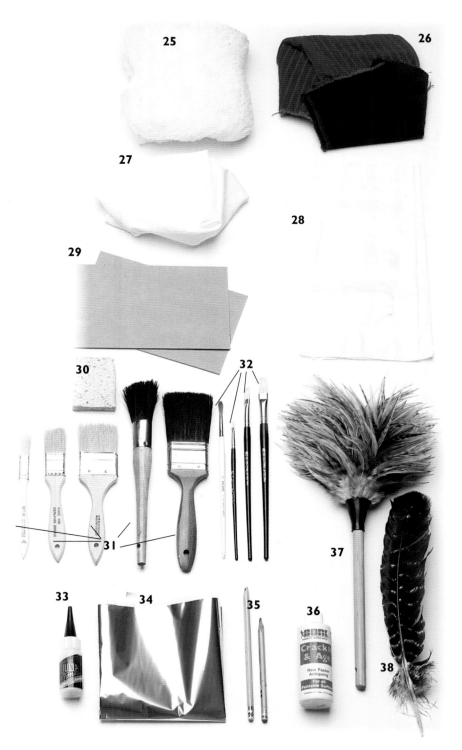

1. Paint tray
2. Paint can for mixing and storing paints and glazes
3. Disposable bowls for holding paints and glazes
4. Paper plates to use as disposable paint palettes and as an imprint tester
5. Plastic container for mixing and storing paints
6. Paint roller
7. Paint roller covers
8. Paint stirrer
9. Plastic spoon—use back to rub masking tape guidelines firmly in place
10. Paint scraper and pads
11. "Car-wash" sponge
12. Level for checking guidelines
13. Paint pads—available in various sizes
14. Metal graining combs
15. Sea sponges
16. Fume-filtering masks with special filters
17. Plastic surgical gloves
18. Round brushes
19. Disposable foam brushes
20. Dust and particle filtering mask
21. Masking tape—available in many widths and degrees of tackiness
22. Electric tool for cutting stencils
23. Craft knife for cutting stencils
24. Stenciling spray adhesive to keep stencils in place while you work
25. Cheesecloth
26. Corduroy
27. Cotton rags
28. 1-mm thick plastic drop cloth
29. Sandpaper—available in many grades from coarse to fine
30. Household sponge
31. Brushes in several widths
32. Artist's brushes
33. Adhesive over which to apply metallic foil
34. Silver foil
35. Chalk pencil and standard pencil for marking guidelines
36. Ready-mixed crackle glaze
37. Feather duster
38. Large feather

CHAPTER THREE

PREPARING TO PAINT

Contrary to what you might think, the difference between a professional painted finish and an amateur attempt isn't always a matter of technique.

Where professional painters put their time and effort—for the biggest pay-off—is in surface preparation. In fact, they often budget more time for this than for the actual painting, just to get the perfect "canvas" for their work.

That's because they know from experience that in decorative painting each layer builds on the previous one to create that great final effect. Without care and neatness in your prep work, your surface can become a distraction, drawing attention to its imperfections rather than your handiwork. Worse yet, poor preparation can even cause your finish to peel off or crack soon after you've completed it.

Figure in prep work time as soon as you choose your project. How much time will depend on the size of your project and the condition of your surfaces. For instance, readying an entire room, with surfaces in good condition, can take several days. Some tasks, like scraping and sanding, are painstaking; other tasks, like washing down walls, require drying time.

If your surfaces are in particularly poor condition, or if the job is especially large, you may want to do what many professional decorative painters do: Hire an interior house painter to complete this crucial stage.

Your decision will, of course, be based on budget considerations, too. But keep in mind the time involved—yours might be more profitably spent on other things. It will also probably take an experienced pro, already familiar with tools and materials needed for various projects, less time.

Stripping wallcovering is a good example. Practice provides an edge here: What an experienced stripper can do in a few days might take a first-time do-it-yourselfer more than a week—after which you might not have much time, or as much enthusiasm, for your decorative painting.

If you decide to hire someone, you can use this chapter to help you decide what needs to be done, how long it will take, and the best way to communicate your needs to a painter. You can diagnose the condition of your surfaces, get an idea of effective treatments, then compare them to your painter's advice to be sure you get the quality of preparation your project demands. Give weight to your painter's advice. In preparation, practice counts more than theory. Each job is different, and sometimes past experience is the best guide.

Not all projects will require the same level of preparation. It depends on:
■ the surface on which you'll paint (new or old, painted or unpainted, porous or nonporous)
■ the paint you'll use (oil- or water-based)
■ the painted finish you've selected (Some, like ragging, hide imperfections much better than dragging, which needs a super-smooth surface.)

What is preparation work? A multi-step process that can involve cleaning, caulking, skim-coating, sanding, priming, and base-coating your surface. Depending on surface conditions and the finish you choose, you may skip or touch briefly on some steps. New walls, for instance, should require no cleaning except a light dusting and little or no caulking.

Note that the order in which you perform some of the steps varies for different surfaces. For example, unpainted wood, drywall, and plaster must be primed before sanding to seal them and keep them from getting scratched. But painted wood, drywall, and plaster must first be caulked and then sanded to roughen the old paint so that primer will adhere. See the chart at the end of this chapter for the order in which to perform the steps on various surfaces. Descriptions of each preparation step follow.

**In decorative painting, each layer builds
on the previous one.
Great-looking finishes result
from exceptional attention to detail
in the surface-preparation stage.**

Stripping Furniture and Woodwork

This kitchen gleams due to the fact that it was stripped down to the wood before it was painted.

For painted furniture and woodwork in good condition, you can skip stripping and start sanding (see page 44). With old pieces and flea market finds, however, this is not often the case. You will probably need to remove the varnish and paint before you can create a surface suitable for decorative painting. You then prime, caulk, and sand the piece as you would for raw wood.

This is time-consuming work; so before you start, make sure the piece you plan to paint is structurally sound. Move it from side to side; lean on it; pay special attention to its legs and any moving parts, such as drawers or extension leaves. In many cases, you can repair a piece with problems; but if chances for a "full recovery"

are "iffy," your best bet may be to find another object for your attention. And make sure the piece you choose will fit in the space in your home you've set aside for it (can it fit through the doorway, etc.).

There are several ways to strip wood: You can have it done professionally, perhaps by the dipping process in which pieces are placed in a tank of chemical stripper. You can do it yourself with a scraper and one of the many chemical strippers available at home centers and paint stores. Or you can use a scraper and a heat gun.

Note that although a heat gun can save time, you must practice with it first to avoid scorching surfaces. Check home-repair guides for instructions and safety measures.

With chemical strippers, read the manufacturer's instructions very carefully before opening the can. Many strippers contain strong solvents; so heed all safety precautions: Work in a well-ventilated area; wear goggles to protect your eyes from flying paint chips or splashing solvent; wear the kind of safety mask that guards against fumes as well as particles (see photo, page 36); and use chemical-grade rubber gloves to protect your hands (not surgical gloves—strippers will dissolve them).

Strippers soften paint and varnish so that they can be scraped off easily. Liquid gel stripper, which comes in cans, is particularly effective. Dip an old brush into the can and paint a strip about 6-inches long on your surface. Apply another 6-inch strip and continue in this manner. Use the widest brush that will fit in the can. Don't stroke back and forth—it reduces the effectiveness of the stripper.

See the manufacturer's instructions for the time the stripper takes to work after it is applied. Test a small patch to see if paint comes off easily. If it does, scrape it all off with a wide compounding knife, wiping the knife after each pass. Stubborn finishes may require a second coat.

Cleaning

This simple step is vital. It removes dirt from a surface so that paint can bond with it. Whether your surface is painted or unpainted, new or old, will determine how to clean it. For example, if you have new walls, just dust them, wipe them with a soft cloth, or use the soft brush attachment of a vacuum cleaner. For older painted walls and other surfaces in fairly good condition—a little peeling, a few small holes—it's a good idea to wash off any grease, smoke, or dust that has accumulated.

Scraping

Don't remove paint from a surface unless it is absolutely necessary; the job is too difficult and time-consuming. But for old surfaces in poor condition you'll begin the cleaning process by scraping paint from them instead of washing them.

Hold a compounding knife at a 45-degree angle, or a triangle scraper (see drawing, page 46) with blade perpendicular to your surface, and drag it along. Apply firm pressure and keep scraping until you hit a spot where the paint holds well. Skip this area and move to the next. You can use the same technique—but pressing lightly instead of firmly—to smooth new plaster walls.

Stripping Wallpaper

Even if the quality of the walls underneath is particularly poor, you are probably best off removing wallpaper rather than painting over it. The reason: The wallpaper could eventually peel off and ruin your finish.

To remove wallpaper, first test if it can be removed dry, an occasional occurrence. In most cases, however, you start by soaking walls thoroughly with a large brush and hot water. This may take several applications. You can add a commercial wallpaper-stripping compound to the water for extra power. Then, with a compounding knife, strip the paper off, working across rather than down the wall.

To remove several layers of paper, rent a steam stripper. This machine boils water and produces steam that softens wallpaper paste quickly. Starting at the bottom of the wall, soften a strip and then scrape it off with a wide compounding knife.

Sanding

Sanding evens surfaces so that they are smooth to the touch. It also helps paint bond with a surface. There are many grades of sandpaper, for a wide range of jobs—00 grade paper for sanding floors, 600 grade for smoothing varnish, and up to 1200 grade for fine work. Check with your local paint or hardware store for the grade your surface requires.

To sand evenly, use a sanding block (see drawing). You can buy one, usually a wood or rubber block with a handle. Sometimes it comes with a long pole, which makes big jobs less tiring. You can also make a sanding block by taping sandpaper to a piece of two-by-four or a child's block.

Electric sanders are available, but be sure to use them carefully. They tend to move fast and can quickly make a surface uneven if handled improperly. Practice first. Beginners will find them easiest to use on small horizontal surfaces, such as dresser- or tabletops.

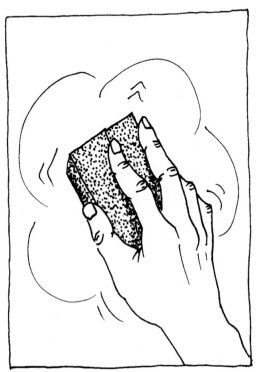

Priming

Primer seals surfaces from dirt, fungus, and humidity. It saturates them with paint so that they can take on colors. And it makes them nonporous so that you'll need fewer coats of paint to get the color you want.

There is a primer for almost every surface, from laminate to glass to brick. Some primers are fire retardant. Others, designed for exterior work, help combat the effects of adverse weather. There are metal primers that prevent rust and help paint adhere to slick surfaces. (See the chart at the end of this chapter for recommended primers for various surfaces.) If you want to apply decorative paint to an unusual surface, ask your home center or paint store which primer to use.

Primer comes in three types: water-, oil-, or alcohol-based. This makes priming a good stage at which to decide on a paint system—water or oil—to work with. (See Chapter Two, *Paints and Tools*, for a review of each system.) Your choice depends very much on the decorative-painting technique you select and the surface you'll be painting on. Furniture, for instance, is done in oils because of their greater durability. If you know which finish you're going to use right now, turn to the recipe for it in Part Two of this book, and see whether its chart recommends water- or oil-based paints.

If you haven't picked a recipe yet, but must continue prep work now, remember this: *You can apply oil- or water-based paints over water- or alcohol-based primers, but only oil paints over oil primer.* In addition, most of the recipes in this book call for a water-based base coat of latex interior house paint. So, play it safe, and start with either a water- or an alcohol-based primer. But first, of course, be sure your surface is compatible with these types. Consult the chart at the end of this chapter or check with your local paint store.

Primer is usually white, which is fine in most cases. In general, the lighter your undercoats, the nicer your finish.

Pale undercoats bring more light into a color and make it richer, while dark undercoats can dull it. Renaissance masters knew this well; they used light washes of color to give their paintings a glow.

But if you plan a dark base coat, you may want to darken your primer to make coverage easier. You can have it tinted at a paint store. For instance, red paints don't always cover well; by having your primer tinted light pink, you're closer to the color you desire for a base coat and may even need one less coat to achieve it. You can also tint primer yourself with artist's oils or acrylics, depending on the type of primer—oils for oil, acrylics for water-based.

Most primers come in both interior and exterior grade. In almost all cases, you'll want interior grade. (Refer to the chart at the end of this chapter to see if your surface is an exception.)

One primer—shellac—comes only in interior grade. It is alcohol-based and available in three colors: white, which dries transparent; blond, which has an orange tint; and a shellac-and-chalk combo commonly called "chalk-tinted shellac," which dries white.

Shellac is one of the best primers for decorative painting because it dries to the touch in about 15 minutes and can be recoated in about a half-hour. Check the label of the product you buy for precise drying times. Because it dries so fast, however, you may have difficulty smoothing out brush or roller marks. Also, it can't easily be sanded down. So put it on with a fine roller and do not go back over it. Disposable rollers are particularly

recommended with shellac because it is hard to clean. If you must clean tools or wipe up spills, use denatured alcohol. Wear a mask that protects against toxic vapors (not just particles, see page 34) when working with shellac.

Shellac is particularly good for sealing plaster. It dries quickly, cutting down on lost time between coats. If, for instance, you used an oil-based primer, you'd have to wait up to 12 hours between coats and apply three or four coats because the plaster absorbs so much primer. But with shellac, you'd need only two coats.

A word about metal primers: There are rusting and nonrusting metals, and each has its own primer. For example, iron, which rusts, either comes factory primed or needs a rust-proofing primer-sealer, which is usually gray or orange.

In addition to preventing rust, it dries fast and provides a surface to which paint can easily adhere. Aluminum, on the other hand, doesn't rust, but it does need a primer that helps paint bind to its surface. Both primers emit extremely toxic fumes, so wear a mask designed to protect against them while you work.

Surface preparation is most important in the bathroom, where surfaces face daily exposure to dampness and humidity.

Spackling

Many surfaces need spackling. Also known as caulking, the process involves filling holes, cracks, and nicks with a spackling compound, plaster of paris, or a mix of the two. There are many ready-mixed spackling compounds on the market today. They come in cans, tubes, or tubs. For best results ask your paint store what professional painters use.

When spackling a crack in an old wall, you must fill it properly so that it won't soon reappear in your freshly painted surface. First, insert a triangular scraper into one end of the crack; then, run the scraper along the crack, enlarging it evenly to about 1/8-inch deep. Wipe the crack with a damp sponge. Apply spackling compound in two or three coats, letting it dry between applications so that the compound will hold better.

Because the compound shrinks as it dries, overfill the crack. If the compound forms a bump, you can sand it smooth after it dries, then dust the surface with a soft brush. Apply primer over any areas you have spackled. (Shellac primer is recommended for this because it dries fast.) The primer will prevent filled holes and cracks from appearing as dull spots in your painted finish.

After you've spackled and sanded, dust the surfaces and vacuum the floor so that dust doesn't get into your paint. You can also sprinkle water on the floor to trap the dust, then sweep it up with a broom. To dust walls thoroughly, painters often use a hand broom.

For furniture, they use a tack cloth, a slightly sticky cloth available in hardware and paint stores. (It is best to use it gently because it can leave a film on surfaces.) An alternative to a tack cloth is a plain, clean cotton cloth dampened with water.

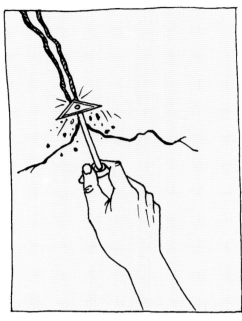

1. To fill a crack, first enlarge it evenly with a triangular scraper to about 1/8 inch. Cut a dovetail-shaped groove so that spackling compound will fill it securely.

2. Before applying spackling compound, wipe crack with damp sponge or mist with spray bottle. Then, scoop compound from container onto large compounding knife, scrape a bit of compound at a time onto a smaller knife, and fill crack.

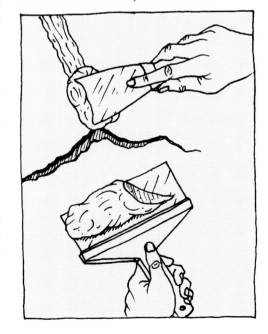

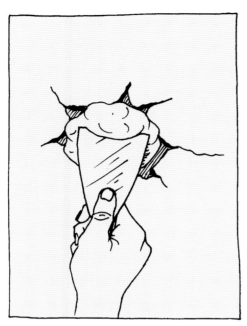

3. For round crack, push compound into center to fill it.

4. Next, work compound out to edges. Let compound dry, then sand it flush with surface.

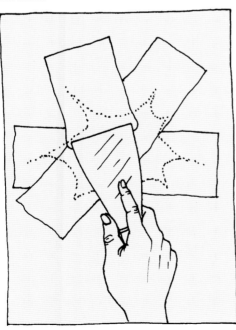

Skim-Coating

After your surfaces are caulked and primed, step back and examine them. Now that they're all one color, you can see what you have to work with. Keep in mind that their condition will strongly influence how your decorative finish will look. Hold a light up to a surface, and its imperfections will become apparent.

For some finishes, especially a gloss or high-gloss like moire or realistic marbling, your surface may still not be smooth enough. In that case you can skim-coat it. This process is difficult and time-consuming—and thus best done by a professional—but it will give you a very smooth surface.

Skim-coating is done over the primer (see drawings, page 48). Because it is a thin coat of spackle, you probably won't have to reprime afterward unless you've applied several skim coats to obtain a smooth surface. This isn't advisable, however. The more skim coats you apply, the weaker your surface becomes and the more likely it is to crack.

You skim-coat with spackling compound. Hold a large spackling knife flat and run it lightly over the walls, filling in any gaps and dents with spackle. Working in 3-foot sections, apply the compound in a long sweep. Then clean off the knife and drag the clean blade back over the surface; the spackling will remain.

Skim-coating is frequently used for flat surfaces like walls, tabletops, and wood furniture. Say you strip, prime, and sand a piece to prepare it for marbling, but its wood grain shows through too strongly. You can skim-coat it following the length of its grain and dragging the knife over the surface at a slight angle so that you fill only the grain. Sand again, and apply a second skim coat, if needed.

TAPING A CRACK

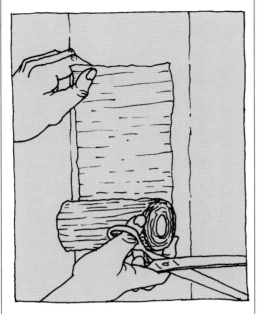

1. Even a carefully filled crack can reappear over time. For extra protection, tape the crack after filling it. Once the fill crack is dry, cover a thin coat of compound with gauze, and flatten it to set it.

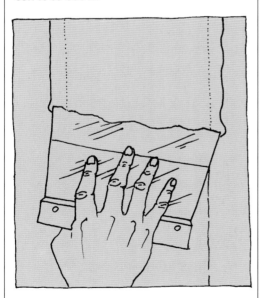

2. After sanding smooth, skim-coat (*skim-coating means applying a thin coat of spackle*) with a wide compounding knife over the gauze to cover it.

SKIM-COATING A WALL

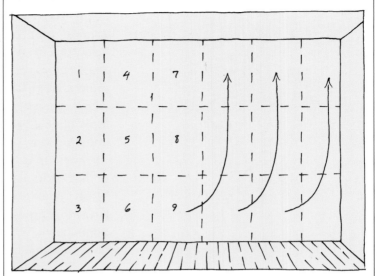

This diagram illustrates how to skim-coat a wall. Work in sections about 2 feet by 3 feet, starting in the top left-hand corner if you are right-handed or the top right-hand corner if you are left-handed. Move down the wall in vertical rows.

PAINTING A ROOM

When painting a room, follow the order professional painters use: Start with the ceiling, then do the walls, window trim, doors and door trim, cornice moldings, fireplace, baseboards, and floor. When doing a floor, work out toward the door so that you don't paint yourself into a corner.

Base-Coating

At this point, select from Part Two the recipe you will execute. Read the chart for that recipe to see if your base coat should be oil or latex. (In most cases, it will be latex.)

Also decide on your base coat and glaze colors now. If you'd like to reproduce a painted finish in the same colors used in its recipe, it will be easier to give the formulas provided under "Base Coat" and "Glazes" in the back of the book to the paint store and have the colors mixed from that.

If you prefer another color combination, first look at paint charts. With the wide range of colors available today, you may well be able to find the base-coat color you want ready-mixed. If not, you can buy a small amount of the color closest to what you'd like and lighten, darken or otherwise alter it with universal tints, which come in many colors and can be used with oil-and water-based paints. When you get the color you want, you can paint a sample on a board, take it to the paint store, get it color-matched, and have larger quantities mixed.

Before you do, however, pick and mix samples of your glaze colors. Paint several sample boards with your base-coat and glaze colors using the technique you've chosen. Study them in various lights to see if you get the color you want. For more on mixing paints, see Chapter Four. (A detailed guide to mixing base coats and glazes is available in the first volume of *Recipes for Surfaces*, page 73.)

After adjusting the colors as needed, you are ready to apply your base coat. In all cases, it should comprise of at least two coats of paint.

For surfaces larger than a set of double doors, apply base coats with a roller. For smaller surfaces, use a brush.

Apply base coats in criss-cross fashion, especially on flat surfaces like panels, doors, and tables. Paint down first, then across, then down again with a brush that is almost free of paint. (Note: Don't paint top and bottom edges of wood doors. This lets wood breathe and prevents warping.)

Criss-crossing is simple with a brush, but not as easy with a roller. With water-based paints—which, because they dry faster, tend to leave brush or roller marks—work in 4-foot sections and go over the second layer in the same direction with a dry roller while the paint is still wet.

Before starting a large project that requires several gallons of paint, pour the paint from all the 1-gallon paint cans into a 5-gallon bucket (available at paint and hardware stores) or a plastic garbage can. Mix thoroughly, then pour paint back into the 1-gallon cans until needed. This extra effort helps insure satisfying results. Despite color differences among paint batches, you'll get exactly the same hue throughout your project.

Paint taken directly from the can is too thick to work with. Although it covers well, it also drips, leaves marks, and dries slowly. For a smoother finish and shorter drying time between coats, thin your first coat 10 to 15 percent with the appropriate solvent (water for latex, thinner for oil). Add solvent a bit at a time so that paint doesn't get too thin. (If it does, leave it out uncovered until the solvent evaporates.) Stir the paint well, and test its consistency with a brush.

Thin your second coat so that it is almost as thin as your first—but never thinner, or the paint will crack when it dries. Wait until the first coat is completely dry. Give yourself plenty of time in which to finish your project. Whenever possible, let each coat dry before applying the next one.

Applying a Base Coat: Step-by-Step

1. **Before using roller to apply base coat to primed wall, paint edge of wall next to molding with flat base-coat brush (about 2 inches). Rolling paint evenly to moldings is impossible; "cutting" a line provides straight edge from which to work.**

2. **Always work from top of wall down, to avoid dripping paint on freshly coated surface. Once edges are trimmed, you can fill in rest of wall using roller.**

3. **To base-coat door, start with panels. Dip brush into paint, coating well. Discharge brush by painting three vertical strokes on top panel. Next, without re-dipping brush, work first from left to right, then top to bottom, and left to right again in criss-cross fashion to smooth paint and prevent color variations. Do lower door panel in same manner; then paint horizontal members, then vertical members, and finally door frame.**

4. **With slanted 2-inch brush, tackle chair rail. As with any surface, paint moldings from top down to prevent drips on just-coated areas. After chair rail do baseboards.**

5. **Do floor last. Sand surface smooth.**

6. **Before you begin painting floor, tape baseboards once they have dried to keep floor paint from getting on them.**

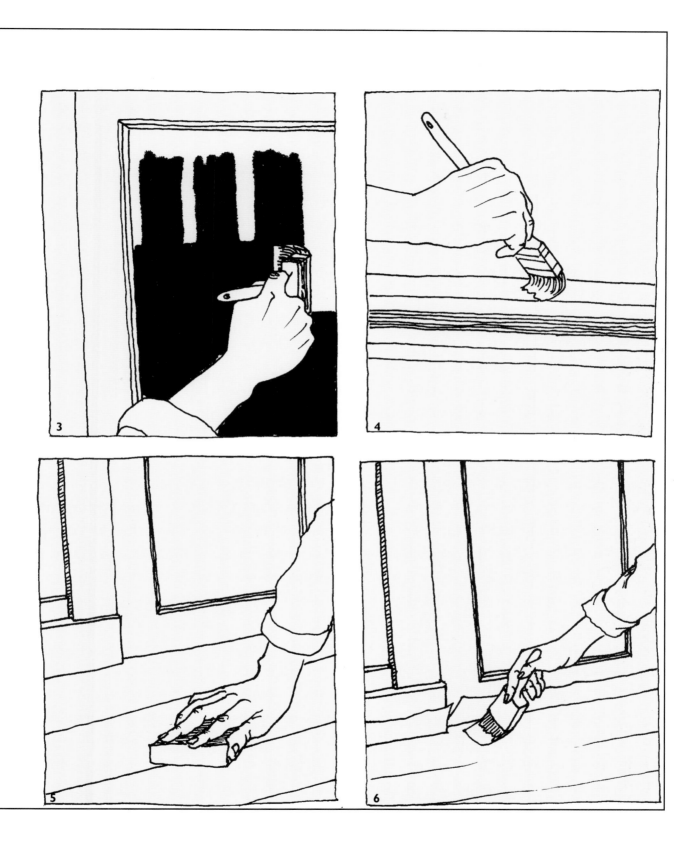

Dividing a Wall into Panels

On many of the recipes, you'll see that a finish is recommended not just for walls, but for wall panels. Marbling, for example, is especially effective presented that way.

The two illustrations show one of many ways you can divide a fireplace wall into panels. Keep in mind that a variation of this pattern might better suit your particular wall.

Draw your design to scale on graph paper first. Start drawing from the center of the wall and work out. Then transfer your design to the wall using a chalkline to "snap" on first the vertical lines and then the horizontals. (See next page for how to use a chalkline.)

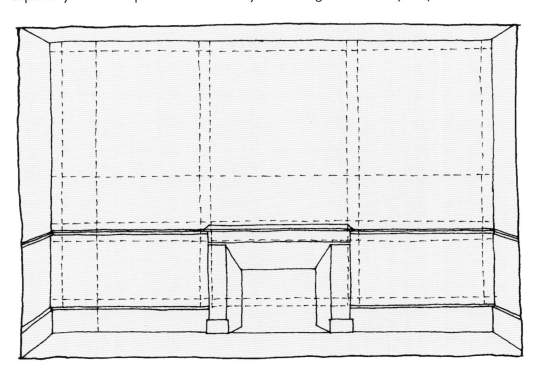

Here is the finished drawing transferred to the wall. Walls divided into panels are often wood-grained, usually in more than one type of wood for an inlaid look. Try "figured" graining (done with a graining tool) for the panels and straight graining (done with a graining comb) for the frame.

Painting a Chair

Note that one of the recipes in this book ("Crackle Glaze," page 157) is demonstrated on a chair. In general, painting furniture will take longer than any other project. That's because of all the curves and angles—and surface imperfections are both easier to create and more noticeable on these smaller surfaces. And since most furniture is painted in oils and varnished for durability, imperfections tend to stand out due to the high sheen the paints give the surface.

Applying paint to a chair can be tricky for novice painters, since most of us have gained our painting experience on large, flat expanses, like walls. The key is to paint one element at a time—each leg of the chair, each side rail, apron, etc.—without getting paint on any other part. If paint does lap over from one element to the next, you must wipe it off immediately. That extra paint would cause an uneven surface if you let it dry and painted over it.

To help keep you neat, paint elements first from one edge toward the center, then from the other edge in, blending paint in the middle. Use a small flat brush scaled to the size of your project for main areas and a soft, pointed sable brush on carved areas, if needed.

Loading and Holding Brushes and Rollers

BRUSHES Pour paint from the large storage container into a smaller bucket. This lets you keep most of your paint covered so that it doesn't dry or form a skin on top. In addition, if debris falls into your open paint bucket, the rest of the batch will not be contaminated. Dip your brush into the bucket so that about two-thirds of the bristles are covered with paint. Then wipe the brush on the inside edge of your bucket to prevent drips. For priming and basecoating, hold your brush at a slight angle and apply moderate, even pressure.

Grasp the brush low on the handle near the bristles for a firm grip. Avoid using excessive pressure, even in corners and other hard-to-reach places; this could damage the bristles of your brush.

ROLLERS Fill a roller tray so that no more than half its ribbed bottom is covered with paint. Dip the roller into the paint at the shallow end of the tray and work it back and forth a few times above the paint line to remove excess paint and prevent drips. Place the roller against the wall, and roll it over the surface in long, even strokes.

HOW TO USE A CHALKLINE

Chalklines let you mark easily erased straight lines on large surfaces. You can buy chalklines at home centers, hardware stores, and paint shops. They are small boxes containing 50 to 100 feet of string on a reel. Some of them need to be filled with chalk or talcum powder; others however, come filled with blue chalk that is difficult to wipe off. If you get one of these, empty it out and refill the box with a mix of three-fourths talcum powder and one-fourth blue chalk. The line produced will be more visible on light surfaces yet easy to remove with a damp cloth.

You'll need a partner—one to hold the box, the other to hold the end of the string. Stretch the string along the surface to be marked, pulling the string tight so it is taut and flat against the surface. Then one person should snap the string hard by pulling it 2 to 3 feet off the surface and letting it go so that when the string hits the surface, it leaves a powdery line.

How to Prepare Surfaces

MATERIAL	CLEANING	PRIMING, SANDING, CAULKING, SKIM-COATING	BASE COAT
Raw wood (old furniture, stripped; new furniture and moldings, unpainted; doors, paneling, cabinetry)	1. Dust lightly with hand broom or soft-brush attachment on vacuum cleaner.	1. Seal knots in wood with shellac. 2. Prime surface to harden pores and seal wood. If you don't know wood species, or if it is tropical wood, use shellac. For other wood, oil-base primer recommended (but latex primer also an option). 3. Sand primer, dust surfaces, sweep area. 4. Caulk and skim-coat, if needed, with spackling compound. 5. Sand surface lightly, dust surface, sweep area.	Oil-based paint recommended for wood. Latex can be used only over shellac or latex primer. Note: On small surfaces such as furniture, apply with brush instead of roller.
Painted wood (furniture, doors, paneling, molding, etc.)	1. Wash with industrial-strength detergent if very dirty. 2. Let dry about a day. Note: Test detergent on small area first to see how it affects painted surface. 3. Scrape, if needed.	1. Caulk areas of painted surface in poor condition. 2. Skim-coat, if necessary. 3. Touch up caulked and skim-coated areas with primer to seal them. Prime any areas where raw wood has been exposed. (You need not prime over painted wood in good condition.) Note: Kind of primer to use depends on paint already on surface. If latex, use oil or latex primer. If oil, use oil primer. If you're not sure, use oil.	Use oil or latex, depending on primer you used and technique you've chosen.
Unpainted drywall (walls)	1. Dust lightly with hard broom or soft-brush attachment on vacuum cleaner.	1. Caulk and skim-coat, if you want very smooth finish. (If you apply more than two skim coats, reprime.) 2. Prime: Shellac recommended, but oil-based or latex primer can be used.	Oil or latex, depending on primer used and technique chosen. Note: Oil-base coat can be applied over all three primers, but use latex base coat only over latex or chalk-tinted shellac combination primer.

How to Prepare Surfaces

MATERIAL	CLEANING	PRIMING, SANDING, CAULKING, SKIM-COATING	BASE COAT
Painted drywall (walls)	1. Wash with industrial-strength detergent if very dirty. 2. Let dry about a day. Note: Test on small area first to see how detergent affects painted surface.	1. Caulk, if needed, to fill holes and cracks. Touch up caulked areas with primer. 2. Skim-coat if you want very smooth finish; then prime. 3. Depending on condition of painted surface, and if you'll paint light color over dark one, you may want to seal whole area with coat of primer. (See "Painted wood, *Priming*," page 54, for kind to use.)	Oil or latex, depending on primer used and technique chosen.
Unpainted plaster (new walls, architectural details, ornaments, sconces, pedestals, capitals, etc.)	1. Dust new plaster lightly with soft-bristle brush. Dust old plaster with hard-bristle brush. 2. Sand flat surfaces lightly, only if needed, taking care not to scratch surface. 3. Dust with soft-bristle brush.	1. Caulk, if needed, with plaster of Paris. 2. Prime with few coats of blond or chalk-tinted shellac. For shellac, use disposable roller or brush, depending on surface size. Note: For small carved surfaces, apply several coats of oil-based primer, thinned.	Oil-based recommended to seal surfaces from humidity, but latex can be used.
Painted plaster (old walls, architectural details, ornaments, sconces, pedestals, capitals, etc.)	1. Wash with industrial-strength detergent if very dirty. Wash around spots of exposed raw plaster. 2. Let dry at least two days, especially if paint is chipped and water seeps into plaster.	1. Caulk, if needed, to fill holes and cracks. Touch up areas with primer. 2. Skim-coat if you want very smooth surface; then prime. 3. Depending on surface condition, and if you're painting light color over dark one, you may want to seal whole area with coat of primer. Note: Kind of primer to use depends on paint already on surface. If latex, use oil or latex primer. If oil, use oil primer. If you're not sure, use oil.	Oil-base recommended to seal surfaces from humidity.

How to Prepare Surfaces

MATERIAL	CLEANING	PRIMING, SANDING, CAULKING, SKIM-COATING	BASE COAT
Laminates, plastics, and resins (kitchen cabinets and counters, appliances, tabletops, pedestals, capitals, light fixtures, etc.)	1. Wipe down with denatured alcohol. 2. Wash with industrial-strength detergent, rinse well, let dry.	1. Roughen surface by sanding with 150-grade sandpaper. 2. Apply "surface duller" such as acetone. (Wear gloves, goggles, and mask, and take safety precautions with these flammable solvents.) 3. Prime with plastic-grade primer.	Oil base recommended for durability and compatibility with oil-based primer. Note: Read manufacturers' labels on primers. Some water-based primers can be used with an acrylic base coat (more durable than latex) and varnished well.
Canvas (canvas No.10 cotton cloth recommended for floor cloths)	None.	1. For large floorcloth, you can stretch canvas by stapling it to wall, but you will need scaffolding to work on it. Place inexpensive fabric and plastic sheet behind canvas to cushion canvas and create smooth surface for sanding. 2. Sand canvas lightly. 3. Prime canvas with gesso acrylic primer, available in art supply shops, or with standard latex primer. Apply two coats. Thin first coat about 30 percent and second coat about 10 percent.	Two base coats of latex paint.
Other fabrics (T-shirts, curtains, etc.)	1. Wash, iron, and press, if necessary.	None.	Textile paint using, special brushes with stiff, short hair, available in art supply shops.
Paper (posterboard for samples— hot-press with semi-gloss finish recommended)	1. Dust lightly, if needed.	1. Prime with shellac and chalk combination or oil-based primer. (Do not use water-based primer.) 2. Sand lightly.	Two coats of oil- or latex-based paint, whichever is used for your technique. Note: In making samples, you can put water-based paints over oil—paper will absorb most of oil and results don't need to be durable.

How to Prepare Surfaces

MATERIAL	CLEANING	PRIMING, SANDING, CAULKING, SKIM-COATING	BASE COAT
Papier-mâché, papers for making your own wallpaper, gift wrap, etc.	1. Dust lightly, if needed.	1. Prime with oil-based primer.	Oil-based paints.
Metal, rusting — iron (furniture, accessories, stair rails)	1. Go over entire surface with wire brush to remove rust, if necessary. 2. Wash new, factory-primed surfaces with detergent.	1. Use rust-proofing primer.	Check manufacturer's labels to see which paints are compatible with primer. In most cases, the paint is oil-based, but some exterior-grade latex paints (more durable than interior-grade) may be compatible.
Ceramic (tubs, lavatories, tiles, old appliances with baked-on ceramic finishes, etc.)	1. Remove protective grease finish from new and unprimed surfaces with acetone. Note: Acetone is flammable and toxic. Take safety precautions: wear mask, goggles, and gloves.	1. Use primer for non-rusting metals to help paint adhere to surface.	Ask your paint store, hardware store, or home center for ceramic-grade spray paint. Make a sample on tile to test paint for adherence and durability.
Metal, non-rusting—aluminum (appliances, cabinets, etc.)	1. Wash with industrial-strength detergent.	1. To roughen surface, sand with heavy-grade paper in circular motion.	Oil-based recommended, but exterior-grade latex (more durable than interior grade) is also compatible with most primers, which are usually alcohol-based.
Glass (table-tops)	1. Clean with spray window cleaner to dissolve grease. 2. For tough jobs, cover surface with layer of powdered cleanser; then wipe off with damp cotton rag to absorb dirt and grease.	None.	Use sign painter's lettering enamel. Paint on underside of glass. Caution: Test paint on glass for durability. Finish can scratch off. Glass is nonporous and, thus, less durable than, say, wood or drywall.

CHAPTER FOUR

MIXING PAINTS

Over the past several years, the increasing popularity of decorative painting has turned it from an art practiced by professionals into a craft do-it-yourselfers have heartily embraced.

One area where this change is most apparent is in mixing paints. Today, there are many more ready-made products on the market that make the decorative-painting experience easier. And the options are still evolving. Spurred by environmental concerns with oil paints and the less-than-earth-friendly solvents they require, companies are developing new water-based products with the best properties of oils while still being safe to use and easy to clean up.

All this leaves you with some decisions to make. The biggest choice is the same one you face in the kitchen. Are you the buy-a-box-of-cake-mix type, or do you believe in doing everything from scratch?

There's no need for guilt here. There are simply two different approaches. You can go to a paint store, pick up the paints you need, and get started on your project. Or, if you want the full experience of decorative painting, you can mix your paints yourself.

As in cooking, both approaches may be right for you at different times. Base your decision on the amount of time you have, your budget, your skill level, and your goals.

For example, if you want to decorate in a hurry, go the ready-made route. However, if you want to devise a truly unique color scheme for your home based on a prized Oriental rug or beloved heirloom, you'll benefit from the full color-mixing experience.

Before you start mixing paints, read Chapter One, *Color*. You can also refer to the first volume of *Recipes for Surfaces* for a detailed guide to what supplies you'll need to get started and how to go about it.

There is, of course, a middle ground. You might want to try customizing your paints by tinting them slightly. To alter a latex base coat or water-based glaze, you can use artist's acrylics or universal tints (but make tints less than 10 percent of your total paint mix or paint won't dry properly).

For an alkyd base coat or oil glaze, you can use japan colors, artist's oils, or universal tints (less than 10 percent of total mix). You may still, however, prefer to go to your local paint store and have color adjustments made (especially to large quantities).

Base Coats

There are several ways to get the base-coat color you want. The simplest involves going to the paint store and having the paints mixed for you.

Colors for the finishes in this book have been selected with many of today's most popular decorating styles in mind. So, in some instances, you may want to reproduce a finish just as it appears. All you have to do then is take this book with you to a paint store or home center and show them the diamond-shaped "paint chip" found under the "Base Coat" section on the recipe card; a similar color can be mixed for you. Or, you can give them the formula listed in the *Recipe Paint Formulas* section of the book, (see pages 182-184,) and have the color mixed from that.

A formula is given for every paint color used in this book. The formulas employ abbreviations and codes that tell how many "squirts" of a particular color go into creating the final hues.

This paint-mixing "language" is an industry standard. But even with the precise formulas, you may still get a slight variation of the colors shown here. This is a reflection of differences in paint brands. (The brand used for the finishes in this book was Benjamin Moore & Co.) However, someone skilled at mixing paints can often compensate for the differences.

If you prefer another color combination, first look at paint charts. With the wide range of colors available today, you may well be able to find the base-coat color you want ready-mixed.

If not, you can buy a small amount of the color closest to what you'd like and lighten, darken, or otherwise alter it with universal tints, which are affordable and easy to use, available in many colors, and compatible with oil- and water-based paints. When you get the color you want, you can paint a sample on a board, take it to the paint store, get the color matched, and have larger quantities mixed.

Before you apply your base coat, refer to Chapter Three, *Preparing to Paint*, for complete instructions.

EXPERIMENTING WITH SAMPLES

Before going any further, base-coat several sample boards in the color you plan to use for your technique so that you can test your glaze on them and get a true impression of what your finished effect will look like.

Paint samples on double-ply, hot-press illustration board. Use boards about 2 feet by 2 feet so that you get a good preview of your finished effect. Prime the boards so that they won't bubble and will absorb paint in the same way as your surface. Use the type of primer (alkyd, latex, or shellac) that is compatible with your base coat (see chart, Chapter Three).

Glazes

In this book, many of the "oil-system" finishes (those executed in oil-based paints) feature a true "glaze" over their base coats—a glaze being distinguished from paint by its transparent quality, which comes from combining paint with glazing medium and solvent.

Some of the oil-system finishes and all the "water-system" finishes shown, however, don't use any glazing medium at all. Over their base coats are either paint applied straight from the can or paint mixed with the appropriate solvent (paint thinner or water).

Your first step in mixing a glaze should be to read the recipe for the dec-orative finish you want to create. Check the recipe chart to find out if you need water- or oil-based glaze or paint, referred to on the chart as an "Applied Finish." Decide if you want to replicate the color in the book or devise one of your own. As with your base coat, if you want to get the exact color of paint (whether used in glazing liquid or alone) in the recipe, you can bring the formula supplied under "Glaze" or "Applied Finish" to a paint store.

A recipe for mixing an oil-based glaze follows. For water-system finishes, instructions for getting paint to the desired consistency using water are noted in the recipe.

Keep in mind, however, that just as in cooking, recipes for glazes are general guides. In cooking, you follow the steps, taking into account variations in, say, cooking time because of oven temperatures and the type of food being prepared. Mixing a glaze is somewhat similar; the process must be adapted to the needs of each technique or surface. Some techniques demand a very translucent glaze; others work best with pure paint. Some surfaces are best served by a thick glaze that won't run.

Because of these variations, you should always read the complete recipe and its chapter introduction before mixing a glaze. That's where you'll find clues to proper consistency and translucence.

Testing, however, is the only way to be sure you've got what you need. The best way to test is to apply glaze over a sample board painted with your base coat (see "Experimenting with Samples," above).

Even with testing, problems can crop up. If your glaze doesn't cover your surface well enough or you find it running, don't panic. First, wipe it off with a clean cloth. Then, only if needed, wipe surface with a cloth dampened with thinner.

Note that there is a counterpart to oil-based glazing liquid for the water-based system, which you might want to try. It is transparent acrylic gel medium, which you mix with water and tint with artist's acrylics or universal tints. (You can find instructions for mixing acrylic glaze in the first volume of *Recipes for Surfaces*, page 82.)

MIXING AN OIL-BASED GLAZE

Mixing a glaze is simple. And there's a simple way to tell if you have it right. Start by mixing up a batch of standard proportions—80-percent glazing liquid and 20-percent paint. Then dip a brush into it, and swipe it across a piece of newspaper. If you can read the print through the glaze, you've got a good level of transparency.

Next, check your glaze's consistency. Ideally on a sample board painted with your base-coat color, but even on plain white paper, use some of the glaze to make imprints with the tool employed in creating your finish (i.e., sponge, rag, comb, etc.) If the imprint is too thick, thin the glaze with paint thinner. But be sure to add just a little at a time, and test as you go. (The thinner will, of course, also make the glaze more translucent.)

Going slow is very important because it's pretty tough to thicken a glaze you've thinned too much. With a small batch of glaze, it's probably best to mix a new batch. For a large amount, you can let it stand open to the air for about 12 hours until most of its diluent evaporates. A skin may form on top of the glaze as it thickens, in which case you'll have to strain it through cheesecloth to remove the skin.

Here are the materials you'll need:

- newspaper or drop cloth to cover your work surface

- rubber gloves

- mask

- newspaper on which to test glaze for transparency; flat bristle brush about 2 inches wide to test glaze with

- plastic container to hold glaze

- paint stirrer

- oil-based glazing liquid

- oil-based paint

Also have ready: the tool you'll use to apply the glaze for the finish you've chosen; paint thinner to further dilute your glaze, as needed; and the tool you'll use for your finish so that you can test the imprint it gives you.

Note that paint thinner isn't the only diluent you can use with oil-based glaze:

- flatting oil, a mix of turpentine, linseed oil, and dryer specially formulated for compatibility with ready-mixed glazes

- turpentine, which causes glazes to dry more slowly than paint thinner does (thus, giving you more time to work a surface)

- kerosene, which is oilier than the others and thus keeps glazes wet the longest

The step-by-step photographs show how to mix a small batch. For the amount of glaze needed for a larger project, see Chapter Two, *Paints and Tools*.

Mixing an Oil-Based Glaze: Step-by-Step

1. Open glazing liquid and mix well; product tends to separate. Fill container with three parts glazing liquid. (Be sure container is big enough to hold rest of ingredients. You don't have to be exact; you can measure by "eyeball" or count as you pour.) Open paint; mix well. Fill final quarter of container with paint. Stir well.

2. Test transparency by painting it over newsprint; if you can read print, glaze is transparent enough. Also test consistency by applying it with tool you'll use for your technique and evaluating imprint. Add paint thinner, if needed, a little at a time. Test after each addition. Don't exceed one-third of mixture.

CHAPTER FIVE

BEFORE
YOU
BEGIN

If you're thinking about diving right in without going through the rest of the book, please at least take just a few minutes to read these pointers before starting your decorative-painting project. It'll save you time, money, and lots of aggravation—while making your painting experience much more fun and your results much more professional. We promise!

Practice...please! More than anything, this is what will give you a professional look. It's also the key to making this creative undertaking a pleasure instead of a strain.

We're not talking long-term commitment here—but the first time you try a technique shouldn't be on your walls. Of course, you can paint over a finish if you're not satisfied with it—that's one of the pluses of decorative painting.

But why waste the time and materials, when a few dry runs on cardboard will let you find out such things as:

- if you really like the colors you've chosen when you see them one on top of the other in their final form ("textured" glaze over base coat)

- if the glaze you've mixed is opaque enough to give you a true decorative painting effect

- just how much pressure to use in applying paint to get the looks you see in the following pages

- just how much paint to apply to your surface to get the look you want

EXPERIMENT! While you're practicing, experiment with everything, especially color. Just consider the colors of the finishes you see in these pages "serving suggestions." Specially selected for their ability to work with today's most popular decorating schemes, these hues are hot in home furnishings and accessories, even ready-to-wear.

But the key is not to let the color a finish appears here limit you and your decorating schemes. This book is just a guide. Perhaps a lighter, darker, or whole new shade would better suit your decor. Don't hesitate to add your own creative input. For inspiration and instruction, see the chapters on *Color* and *Mixing Paints* in this book.

KEEP IT CLEAN! Remember that "foreign particles"—dirt, dust, bristles from brushes, fuzz from cloth rollers—are the enemy of decorative painting. Keeping these elements off your finishes is also crucial to getting a professional look. One good tip: Use foam rollers and brushes instead of cloth rollers and bristle brushes so that you don't end up with fuzz and hairs in your finishes.

Also: Make sure your work environment is clean. Do the prep work—wash down your surfaces, smooth them out, etc.—and then clean up thoroughly, especially after sanding.

WATCH HOW YOU WORK IN PAIRS! Some techniques—the "subtractive" one in which you apply glaze with a roller or brush and then remove it with a tool like a sponge or comb while it's still wet—are more easily executed by two, especially over a large area. But make sure each person keeps doing "the same job" all through the project.

In other words, if you start by rolling on the glaze, and your partner follows behind removing it with a cloth, don't switch in mid-stream. Your decorative painting style is like your signature—unique to you. The amount of pressure you use when you remove glaze, the way you hold the cloth, all impact on the final look of the finish. By switching, you'll end up with two styles on one surface.

READ THAT RECIPE! Before you begin, read the entire recipe for a technique, as well as the introduction to the chapter. You'll find additional color suggestions, tips to make the project easier, and help in correcting results you might not be satisfied with.

As in cooking, be sure you have everything you'll need on hand. Reading the whole recipe first will give you a clear idea of what's needed and how you'll use it so that you can determine quantities for a particular project. A thorough reading will also help you figure out how much time to set aside to complete the recipe.

PAINTING POINTERS

HOW BASE COATS WERE APPLIED. Almost all the base coats in this book have been applied with a roller, using traditional house-painting methods. (Exceptions include the chair and other small objects on which the base coat was either applied with a brush or sprayed on.)

For all the finishes, the base coat must be dry before glaze is applied. Drying times vary; see Chapter Two, *Paints & Tools* for guidelines. *Note that, in most cases, the recipes start at the point where you have a dry base coat and are ready to apply your glaze.*

HOW GLAZES WERE APPLIED. With "subtractive" finishes (those that involve removing glaze), glaze has usually been applied with a roller. In some instances, however, it was applied with a brush to give the finish added texture or "direction." Note that brush size depends on the size of your project. For example, to glaze a wall in a reasonable amount of time, you'll want to use a brush 4 inches wide or larger.

HOW TO GLAZE IN CORNERS. One of your biggest challenge spots will be in the corners of a room. Excess glaze tends to gather in corners. You can dab some out with a brush or a sponge cut to fit. Dab each spot once, and wipe your tool on a clean cloth every few times.

Your best bet, however, is to paint your walls in this manner: Opposite walls one day, then let them dry overnight. The next day, tape their edges, and paint the two remaining walls.

See the drawings on the following pages for the most effective way to glaze a room, as well as how to glaze a wall for both additive and subtractive techniques.

Diagram shows how to glaze using a subtractive technique. One person begins rolling glaze from a top corner (left for right-handed, right for left-handed), working in a 2-to-3-foot-wide strip. After reaching bottom of wall, this person returns to top of wall and begins glazing strip next to it, while other person manipulates wet glaze on first strip.

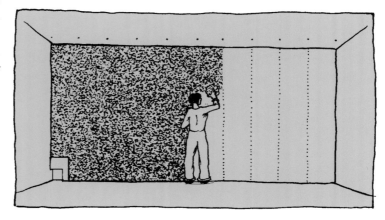

Diagram shows how to apply glaze using an additive technique. Start in a top corner—left one if you're right-handed, right if you're left-handed so that your arm doesn't touch completed work. Move down wall in 2-to-3-foot-wide strip; then go to top of wall and begin new strip next to it. Overlap strips just enough to avoid leaving a space where base coat shows through, but not enough to form dark line between rows.

MASKING

Speaking of tricks to make your life easier, masking is definitely one of them. Using tape to block out areas you don't want paint to get in can go a long way toward helping you achieve professional results. It will keep your work neat; give you clean-edged painted lines that go exactly where you want them to go; and make the classic technique of lining much easier to execute.

Following are examples from the recipes in this book where masking came in handy. Taping the baseboards before rolling glaze over your faux-flagstone floor finish will keep them paint free while letting you get paint coverage right up to the wall edge. Taped lines form the mortar in the "Brick" recipe and create the inlay patterns in the "Granite" and "Malachite" recipes. Taping every other strip lets you grain more easily in the "Moire" recipe.

Equipment-wise, you'll need scissors, masking tape, and a plastic spoon or a credit card. The latter is something you can use to rub the edges of the tape firmly into place—a very important step, and not one to skimp on. If the tape isn't sealed in place, paint could seep under the tape. In fact, even with extensive pressing, this is bound to happen at times. For this reason, you should always keep some of your base coat paint on hand for touch-ups. Using a small, fine artist's brush, you can carefully paint over any drips. You can also use paint thinner for oil paint or denatured alcohol for latex paints on a cotton swab to remove any seepage.

Masking tape comes in many widths, from as small as 1/8 inch, which might be just right for an inlay pattern, to as wide as 3 inches, which could cover over molding. It also comes in several levels of tackiness. For masking, look for "light-tack" or "safe-release" type tapes. These are less sticky and, thus, safer on already painted surfaces. You want a tape tacky enough to keep paint from seeping under, yet easy enough to remove—even after an extended period—so that it wouldn't, say, take the paint off your newly painted moldings. Always test tape in an inconspicuous place first to prevent surprises.

MASKING AN OBJECT

This clock is being prepared for painting with the "Malachite" recipe. You can see the finished version on page 99—if you had to hand-paint a circle around the face of the clock without getting any on the glass, it would certainly change the skill level required for this project. Masking in a circle keeps the project simple. Note that you must use a light-tack masking tape to cover the face of the clock.

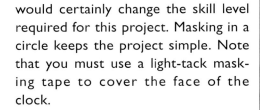

Using 1/8-inch tape, divide surface into sections to form inlay pattern. Align horizontal lines with base of clock. Make sure the tape is pressed firmly onto the surface with a plastic spoon or credit card so that no paint seeps underneath.

KEY WORDS TO KNOW

Additive techniques: One-person techniques in which you make impressions with glaze on a base coat using various tools such as sponges, rags, and brushes. Among these techniques are sponging on and ragging on.

Alkyd paint: Interior or exterior house paint that comprises a mix of alkyd resin and oil. Used today instead of purely oil-based paint because it dries faster and contains no lead.

Artist's acrylics: Paints made from ground pigment bound with acrylic medium, a transparent gel. They dry quickly to a waterproof finish and can be thinned with water. In decorative painting, you can use them for such techniques as marbling and *trompe l'oeil*, as well as to tint latex base coats and water-based glazes.

Base coat: Opaque layers of latex or alkyd paint that dry to a durable finish. In decorative painting, glaze is applied over the base coat.

Blending: Toning down imprints left in glaze by an implement such as a sponge, brush, or cloth to achieve a softer effect or to combine different-colored glazes on a surface. Done by touching the surface with a light, feathering motion.

Cloth distressing: Using materials such as cheesecloth or cotton rags to apply or remove glaze. The most common method of distressing the surface is with material bunched up in your hand, as in the techniques of ragging and cheeseclothing. Material can also be used rolled into a tube, as in rag rolling, or in long strips, as in "Plastic-Wrap Ragging Off."

Combing: Drawing a toothed instrument, such as a graining comb or cardboard with teeth cut into it, through wet glaze produces effects such as "Moire" and naive wood graining.

Composition: In decorative painting, how the light and dark areas of a painted finish or the multiple imprints of your tools form on a surface. You don't want a huge dark spot in one corner of your surface, for instance, because it will distract the eye from the overall look.

Crackle glazing: A way to give painted surfaces the tiny cracks that come with age. Crackle glaze can be bought off-the-shelf in paint or craft stores or mixed from glue size and other ingredients. Crackling occurs because a latex-based product is applied over an oil-based product. This method is related to *craquelure* in which a water-based varnish is applied over an oil-based varnish.

Criss-crossing: Method of applying base coat and glazing smoothly and evenly over a surface. Should always be employed when applying glaze with a brush to minimize brush marks. Begin by painting or glazing from top to bottom, then, without picking up more paint or glaze, go over it from side to side and, finally, lightly from top to bottom until you eliminate brush marks.

Cutting: Thinning pure paint or glazing medium with a diluent such as water or paint thinner to give it a more workable consistency.

Dabbing: Touching surface lightly and repeatedly with a painting tool in quick motions, creating smooth, even marks. You dab with a rag in ragging techniques, with a brush in stenciling techniques.

Decoupage: The traditional technique of gluing cut-out shapes of paper or other material to a surface and then covering the surface with several coats of varnish.

Diluents: Solvents or thinners that dilute paint to workable consistency; i.e. paint thinner for oil-based paints, water for water-based paints.

Dragging: Technique best executed by two people (especially over large areas) in which one person applies glaze with a brush or roller and the other person removes some of the glaze by sweeping over it with a metal graining comb, piece of cardboard with a feathered edge, dry paint brush, or other tool.

Dry brushing: Working with a brush that is almost free of paint. Brush may pick up paint from one part of glazed surface and move it to another, as in the "Rusted Metal" technique.

Dryer: Chemical found in ready-mixed oil-based paints that speeds drying time. Also, chemical liquids such as japan or cobalt dryer, which you can buy in art and paint stores to speed drying time of oil-based paints. Dryer should be added to paint a few drops at a time.

Fade-away: An effect featuring a gradual progression of a glaze color from dark to light or vice versa; or from one color to another. Fade-away can be particularly effective with stenciling.

Fantasy colors: Reproducing natural materials in colors not found in nature, as shown in the "Marble" recipes.

Flogging: A decorative painting technique in which you manipulate the glaze by striking your surface with a long-bristled brush. A special "flogging" brush with 5-inch-long bristles is ideal for executing this technique, but it is costly; instead, you can use a household painting brush with the longest bristles you can find.

Fresco: The age-old art of painting on fresh, still-wet lime plaster using pigments mixed with water. It produces soft, subtle colors and a finish of great depth. The "Fresco" recipe in this book captures the feeling of a frescoed surface using a simple cloth-distressing technique instead of pigments and plaster.

Glaze: Oil- or water-based paint that is transparent because it contains much more glazing liquid or water (depending on type of paint) than pigment. With many of the techniques in this book, the glaze contains just 20 percent paint. Because of this, when applied over a base coat, the glaze's transparency allows the base coat to show through.

Inlay: To decorate a surface by insetting thin layers of fine materials into it. In decorative painting, the "inlay" look is great for faux granite, marble, and malachite. With malachite, for instance, that's the way it's usually seen. Because you work in small sections, painting is easier—shorter distances to keep your hand steady over and the design looking the same. Masking out areas between inlays with tape keeps them free of unwanted paint.

Japan colors: Ground pigment bound in a resin that originally came from a Japanese tree (hence, the name). Favored by sign painters, these concentrated opaque paints dry quickly to a flat finish. They are excellent for tinting oil glazes or adjusting the color of alkyd base coats.

Latex paint: Water-based interior and exterior house paint similar to acrylic. It dries quickly, has little odor, and is available in finishes from flat to glossy.

Marbling: Decorative painting technique that lets you capture the look of marble.

Moire: Silk, rayon, or other fabric with a wavy or watermarked pattern running through it. Chinese water silk is an excellent example, and the basis for the "Moire" technique in this book.

Natural flow: Also referred to as the "direction" of a finish, it means generally heeding the overall natural line and pattern of the material you are reproducing, i.e., the way the veining runs in marble, the way water would flow over a piece of metal and wear paint away naturally.

Palette: 1) A thin oval or rectangular board, or a tablet of disposable sheets, on which you mix small quantities of paint. A traditional palette has a hole in it through which you stick your thumb to hold it. You can, however, also use a paper plate as an inexpensive and readily available alternative to a palette. 2) The group of colors you choose for your decorative finish or room scheme.

Pigment: Powder ground from natural or synthetic material that gives paint its color.

Primer: Sealant that goes under the base coat to protect the raw surface, make it non-porous, and prevent humidity and dirt from seeping in. There are many types of primer—which you use depends on your surface material.

Sample board: A surface on which to practice techniques, experiment with colors, and preview your final effects. Primed 15-inch by 20-inch double-ply, hot-press illustration board is recommended. (Note: This is in addition to the white paper you should have on hand to test imprints of your tools and final colors before they go on your surface.)

Shellac: Alcohol-based primer that dries fast. Depending on the kind you use, it will dry to a clear, amber, or white color.

Smoothing out: Getting rid of brush marks or softening painted lines on a still-wet painted or glazed surface. Move a long, soft-haired brush appropriate for your paint type and project size over surface in soft, feathery motion.

Spattering: Creating a fine array of colored dots on a base coat by various methods including "printing" them on as in the "Spattering" technique and flicking paint off the bristles of a brush.

Sponging: Applying or removing glaze by dabbing a sponge on a surface. One of the most easily mastered and most popular techniques itself, it is also used in marbling, stucco, and many other techniques.

Stencil: Design cut out of cardboard, acetate, or stencil paper. You can buy stencils ready-made or make your own.

Stenciling: Placing a cutout design on a surface and applying paint through it with a sponge, stenciling (or other type of) brush, or even spray paint.

Stippling: Applying paint over a surface with a very light, "staccato" dabbing motion; also the name of a decorative-painting technique that creates a finish with a fine texture of dots on a surface through that light dabbing motion with a rectangular stippling brush.

Stucco: A finish comprising portland cement, sand, lime, and water for exteriors, and fine plaster for interiors. Stucco recipe uses "Sponging" technique to capture effect.

Subtractive techniques: Two-step techniques in which glaze is first applied to surface with brush or roller, then partially removed or moved with tools such as rags, sponges, and brushes.

Texture: In decorative painting, it is not a raised surface, but one that gives the appearance of three-dimensionality by layering glaze colors and applying them with tools that create "textured-like" patterns.

Universal tints: Highly concentrated liquid pigment for coloring oil- or water-based paints, used by professional house painters and decorative painters. Tints contain no dryer and thus should never equal more than 10 percent of total volume of your paint—otherwise, paint won't dry.

Varnish: Final transparent coating used to protect painted finishes. Varnish will determine sheen of finish. It comes in flat to high gloss; pick sheen most compatible with your finish.

Veining: Linear pattern of marble; in addition to using paint brush to simulate it, a feather makes a highly effective veining tool, as seen in "Red Marble" technique.

Verdigris: Appealing, and highly popular, greenish blue-gray finish that develops on copper, bronze, and brass as part of natural aging and weathering processes.

Working dry: Applying thin layer of glaze, just enough to cover surface; or applying bit of pure paint (or paint to which just a little thinner, glazing medium, or water has been added) and working it across surface with brush, rag, or other tool.

Working wet: Applying a lot of glaze, often in several colors, one on top of the other before the previous one dries, so that you can blend colors right on your surface as you work. The effect can be seen in the "Flagstone" and "Rusted Metal" techniques.

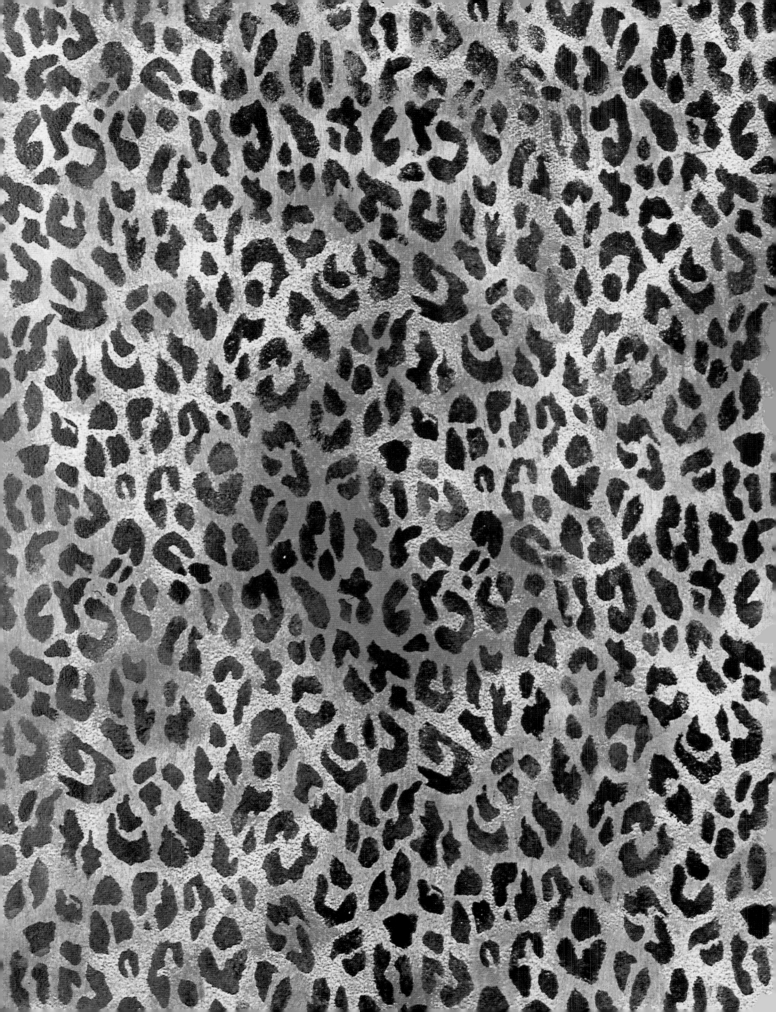

Part Two

THE
RECIPES

CHAPTER SIX

METALS

The trio of techniques in this chapter are great for turning ordinary-looking or out-of-date objects into something special. The accessories you see on these pages were all either lucky finds or bought at garage sales. A change in color was all it took to turn them into perfect complements to a wide range of room settings, or great gifts for special occasions, at a fraction of what they might cost in stores.

There are many more possibilities for including "aging" metal in your decorating schemes than just on accessories. The rich colors of "rusted" metal are a great way to "pick out" the molding in a room with a pale tone-on-tone "textured" wall finish, like those in Chapter Ten. Or, instead of skirting a powder room lavatory to hide the pipes underneath, you might dress up those exposed pipes with an antiqued copper finish.

M E T A L S

If you have an old house and have been viewing those old freestanding metal radiators as eyesores, you might turn them into eye-catching decorative elements with the weathered-bronze effect. A beat-up wooden bed frame, or a plain metal one, could easily be updated and become the centerpiece of a bedroom with any of these recipes.

And don't stop inside. Maybe you've just had the exterior of your house painted; if you have a wrought-iron railing out front, here's a way to refresh that, too. Even gutters and drain pipes are fair game. However, remember that if you use these metal recipes on outdoor surfaces, you must use paint that is compatible with the setting.

Consult your local paint store to make sure your efforts won't crumble under an assault of sun, wind, and rain. And test first: Oil paints sold for exterior use are often much glossier than the paint used here. The sheen won't make much visual sense on your carefully "aged" surface. You might instead be able to use an interior paint topped by a heavy-duty varnish—in which case you'll want a varnish with a flat finish.

However, for a realistic feel, have your brush marks mimic the way water would naturally move over your object—i.e., running down the sides, thus creating vertical streaks in the finish, and puddling up inside, forming a surface pitted in spots where the finish had worn away.

Weathered-metal effects can work great decorative transformations on accent pieces as well as on less-expected elements of your home—like the pipes under your sink!

Before you start your project, study real-life examples of weathered metals, such as the garden faucet on this page. You'll see a great range in shades of color and the patterns they form, which gives you great leeway in creating your own effect.

RECIPE

COPPER VERDIGRIS

LEVEL OF EXPERTISE:

RECOMMENDED ON: Accessories, picture frames, bed frames, moldings, wrought-iron railings

NUMBER OF PEOPLE: 1

TOOLS: Newspaper or drop cloth; mask; rubber gloves; paint thinner for cleanup; rag for touchup; 1-inch round brush; paper to test brush imprint on

 BASE COAT: Metallic copper spray paint or oil-based copper hobby paint in small 2-oz. jars

APPLIED FINISH: Oil-based flat paint

 Seafoam blue

 Seafoam green

VARNISH: No

The aging process is particularly kind to copper and bronze; years of exposure to the elements leave them with a patina of verdigris—that appealing greenish blue-gray finish so popular in home design today. These are some of the simplest finishes to reproduce—and some of the most rewarding because even the beginning decorative painter will be able to come close to the often high-priced verdigris pieces in stores.

This hammered-metal bowl was pulled from a scrap heap and given new life with this recipe. The process began with the application of two coats of oil-based copper-colored paint. Then the "aging" started: dabbing blue and green oil-based paints over top and bottom, with paint concentrated more in some spots than others, then coming back with dabs of copper in places to bring up the background color again.

What makes this finish work so well is its mix of flat and shiny paints. To retain that flat-shiny contrast, and to keep the colors distinct, it's best to let each color dry between applications; otherwise, you'll get a little too much blending.

Even though you're working with oil-based paints, letting the colors dry between applications will be less time-consuming than you think, because the copper paint has a lacquerlike quality that allows it to dry quickly. This fast-drying quality comes at a price, however: strong fumes. So be sure to wear a mask and to work in a well-ventilated room (or outside, weather permitting).

1. Over copper-colored base coat dip 1-inch brush into seafoam blue paint.

2. Dab brush on paper until almost dry. Stipple paint on inside and outside of bowl randomly concentrating paint in spots. Let dry.

3. Dip round brush into seafoam green paint, and repeat step 2. Let dry.

4. Stipple some of copper base coat over green spots to bring up some of background color.

1

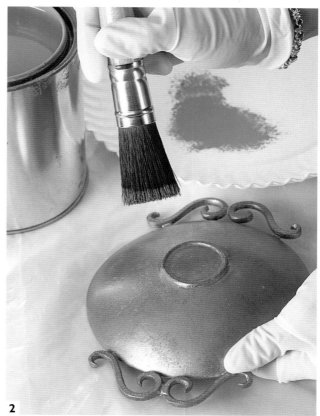

2

3

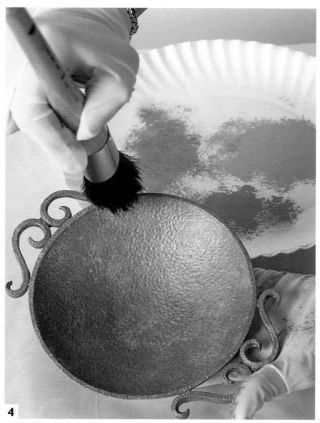

4

RECIPE:

BRONZE VERDIGRIS

LEVEL OF EXPERTISE:

RECOMMENDED ON: Accessories, picture frames, bed frames, moldings, wrought-iron railings

NUMBER OF PEOPLE: 1

TOOLS: Newspaper or drop cloth; mask; rubber gloves; paint thinner for cleanup; rag for touchup; "light-tack" masking tape; 2-inch foam brush for painting base coat; palette; 2-inch bristle brush or old house-painting brush; four "car-wash" or regular household sponges; paper for off-loading excess paint

 BASE COAT: Bronze oil-based semi-gloss

APPLIED FINISH: Oil-based enamel paints—3 shades of green

 Verdigris green

 Sage green

 Pine green

VARNISH: No

A variation of the previous recipe, this one imitates verdigris on bronze—an effect you can easily see for yourself: Just take a look at a photo of the Statue of Liberty.

The wood base and cardboard shade of the candlestick lamp accepted the treatment with equal grace. Done in oils, the finish adhered well to both materials.

To make sure you have the same success with your object, do your surface-preparation work thoroughly. Prep work is what makes all the other paint layers adhere well. Sand your object, if needed, and fill any chips or gauges. Then paint your object with the appropriate primer. (For details, see Chapter Three.)

Again, the combination of a shiny base coat and flat glaze coats makes the look. Note that varnish is an unwelcome addition because it can add an overall sheen to your "well-weathered" surface.

Even though sponges are your main tool in this recipe, it is considered a "dry-brush" technique because of the minuscule amount of paint you use to create it. (Stenciling is another example of a dry-brush technique; it requires about the same amount of paint as this finish.) For best success, use a light touch in applying it, and build the finish up slowly so that the colors don't all run together. That's how you get the depth.

Remember to follow the general direction of the aging process on your piece: Water would run down vertical parts, causing streaks, and pool on horizontal surfaces, which would pit. This directional quality is similar to that discussed in the marbling techniques; you don't need to be a slave to it, but it will add to the realism of your effect.

1. With light-tack masking tape, cover any areas on which you don't want to get paint (in this case, electrical parts, inside shade, edge of cord). Dab dry sponge into first green paint color, then blot off excess on paper, and dab onto lamp. Don't squeeze sponge in your hand. Hold it lightly, parallel to the surface. Apply paint randomly to create light and dark spots. Leave some gaps, which will be filled in with rest of paint colors.

2. Repeat process with two other shades of green. Use brush to push paint into cracks and crevices. Let first color dry before applying second color. Even in oils, this should only take about a half-hour because of how little paint is used.

3. Reapply base coat color in spots to bring up background.

4. Let dry. Remove masking tape. Do not varnish; sheen won't work with "aged effect."

1

2

3

4

RECIPE

RUSTED METAL

LEVEL OF EXPERTISE:

RECOMMENDED ON:
Accessories, picture frames, bed frames, moldings, wrought-iron railings

NUMBER OF PEOPLE: 1

TOOLS: Newspaper or drop cloth; mask; rubber gloves; paint thinner for cleanup; rag for touchup; "light-tack" masking tape; 2-inch foam brush for painting base coat; palette; 2-inch bristle brush and 1/2-inch bristle brush; paper for off-loading excess paint

 BASE COAT:
Walnut brown oil-based enamel paint

APPLIED FINISH: Oil-based enamel paint in 3 colors, plus gold leaf paint

 Rust

 Ebony brown

 Honey

 Liquid gold leaf paint (spray or brush)

VARNISH: No

1. With 2-inch bristle brush, paint gold leaf paint over brown base coat. Do not try for even finish; streaky look is desired. Let dry completely.

2. With 1/2-inch bristle brush, paint a few strips of brown paint, then rust paint, then gold leaf. Work wet —using an up-and-down motion, sometimes starting at top of planter and sometimes at bottom. Overlap your strokes so that some of the colors mix together (but not so they blend into one color).

3. Continue working your way around object, working in small sections several inches wide to keep control of the effect.

Rust can be beautiful—as this metal planter shows. It has the same delicate feel and rich coloration as you might find in tortoiseshell.

The planter is the beneficiary of a blending technique that replicates the effect of rainwater running down the sides of a metal container and puddling inside.

The key here is that you're "working wet"—blending paint colors right on the piece as you go. This is one finish where a streaky look is highly desirable.

Keep in mind, too, however, that like the previous two recipes, this is also a dry-brush technique; so the goal is to use as little paint as possible. In fact, the only real liquid you should need comes from the gold-leaf paint, which contains paint thinner.

You may, however, need to add a bit more thinner to mix the colors to your liking; you can do this by dipping the clean dry brush in thinner and applying it to your surface. If necessary, go back over your surface with some of the paint colors to keep the streaked effect.

Note: Go easy on the walnut brown paint; it can make a piece too dark very fast. It's really the background color and looks best as if peeking through.

4. Smooth over finish with clean, dry brush. Do not over-blend. Finished effect will have naturally streaky look.

CHAPTER SEVEN

STONE

Painted finishes let you capture the spirit of materials you might not otherwise be able to have in your home. For instance, stone can be expensive, because its weight makes transportation costs prohibitive. And weight can also make it unsuitable for your interior without extensive (and costly) shoring up of structural elements.

As with the recipes in the *Reasonable Replicas* chapter, you won't get total realism from these stone effects. But that needn't be the goal. These finishes deliver a more casual, folk-art style, much in keeping with today's preferences for both relaxed design and self-expression in decorating.

When thinking where these effects might work in your home, consider the character you can give a room by painting its floor.

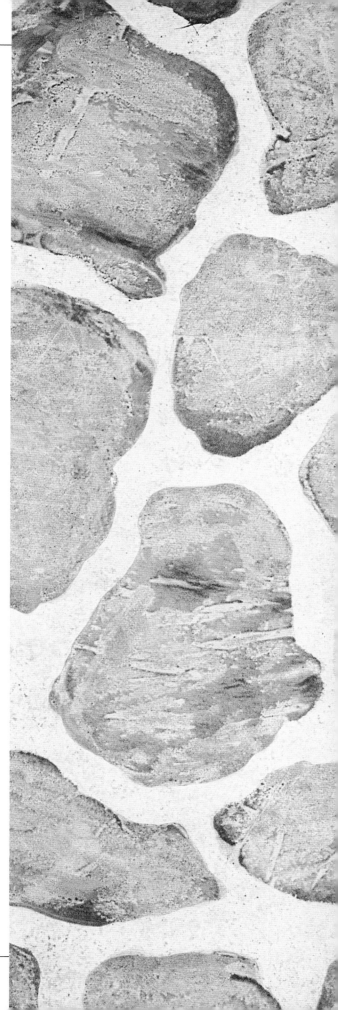

Flagstone, fieldstone, and granite make great options. In an entrance hall, for instance, you can turn the mood formal with a granite inlay-pattern. A flagstone floor in a sunroom can do its part to help bring the outdoors inside.

There is some simple freehand painting involved in some of these techniques. Studying stone patterns will easily give you the hang of the basic stone shapes. Don't try to be exact, and don't be concerned if you make a mistake. That's part of the beauty of decorative painting—if you make a mistake, you can just paint over it and start again.

Note, too, that much of the texture and depth you sense in these finishes *doesn't* come from hand painting; it comes from the tools you use to execute the techniques—sea sponges, newspaper, etc.—and how you apply or remove the glaze.

For a guide to getting floors ready to paint, see Chapter Three, *Preparing To Paint*. For floors in poor condition, paint can be an ideal remedy, as long as you prepare them properly by repairing, stripping, sanding, and priming them.

And remember that when painting a floor you must use the proper type of paint. Review the suggestions in the *Paints and Tools* chapter, and check with your local paint store. Highly durable porch and deck paint is most likely your best choice for the base coat, topped by an oil-based glaze.

You'll also want to apply several coats of varnish for flooring to protect your design. For stone finishes, varnishing is a plus on another level: It brings out the depth and color of the effect and gives it a more genuine feel.

Keep in mind, too, that with floors you must plan to "paint yourself out of the room." You'll end up starting over, of course, if you have to walk over your newly painted finish before it dries.

RECIPE

FLAGSTONE

LEVEL OF EXPERTISE:

RECOMMENDED ON: Floors, fireplace walls, tub surrounds

NOT RECOMMENDED ON: Highly carved surfaces, small surfaces

NUMBER OF PEOPLE: 2 recommended, but can do with 1

TOOLS: Newspaper or drop cloths; roller (with extension handle, depending on project) to apply base coat and glaze; paint trays; paint stirrers; mask; rubber gloves; masking tape to cover areas you don't want painted (like molding); paint containers; paper to test colors on; chalk pencil or chalk to draw outlines of stones; medium-size rounded fitch brush; light-weight plastic sheeting (about 1 mm), cut into wide strips somewhat larger than the size of your stones; "car-wash" sponge

BASE COAT: Maize latex porch and floor paint

APPLIED FINISH: 3 colors of latex porch, deck and floor paint thinned with water; plus gray glazing liquid for final paint coat.

Birch

 Charcoal

Aubergine

 GLAZE: Charcoal oil-based semi-gloss interior house paint

VARNISH: Several coats required for floors

Right off the bat, take our word for it: There's no one precise way of doing this finish. The basic idea is that you don't want two stones of the same color next to each other. You avoid this by creating more colors from the three main paint colors used in the recipe right on your surface.

The colors you'll mix in advance are birch, charcoal, and aubergine. You'll need to mix a third shade of gray right on your surface by combining the two gray paints you already made up. Other shades will be a natural offshoot of "working wet." This means no waiting for paint to dry, or even cleaning your brush, between stone colors—in fact, it's the mixing as you go that gives the depth and richness—and makes you feel especially creative in the process.

In addition to the three colors already mentioned, you may also want to premix brick-red and gray-green colors, shades flagstone often comes in. Or, for a "slate" look, you can execute the technique solely in gradations of gray. And there's always the option of "fantasy" colors geared more to your decor than nature.

With this finish, colors *should* be streaky. That's what gives you the uneven character of the natural stone. But the outlines of the stones should be as neat as possible to give your stones the sharp edges typical of the real thing.

If you're working on a floor, first read the tips in the introduction to this chapter on what kinds of paint to use and what to watch out for. One especially crucial point is to check that the glazing liquid used for your final paint coat is suitable for floors—some are, and some aren't. In any case, you'll need to apply several coats of varnish over your finish to insure long life on this high-use surface.

Before you start on the stone finishes in this chapter, take some time to study the shapes, sizes, and colors of the stones found in venerable old structures like those on page 86.

1. Draw stone shapes on floor with chalk pencil; if you need to make a change, wipe off chalk line with cloth. Then, plan color arrangement of stones so that no two stones of same color are next to one another. Write color name—charcoal, birch, aubergine, etc.— inside outline of each stone.

2. Pour three paints into containers. Note that on a floor, you can't paint all stones of one color first, or you'll eventually have to walk over wet work. Paint in sections. With fitch brush, outline first stone in birch, then fill in. Off-load some paint from brush onto next stone you'll paint, and even next few after that. (The mix with the color you plan to paint those stones will give each stone a slightly unique coloration.)

3. Dip brush into charcoal paint, and paint over second stone (streaks of birch already on it). Stroke some charcoal on first stone you painted, as well as some nearby stones, and work colors while wet to get streaky look.

4. Paint next stone with aubergine, following steps 2 and 3. Continue over surface, using aubergine to form new shades on stones you've already painted as well as stones you have yet to paint.

5. Working with all three colors, complete one section at a time. Let dry thoroughly.

6. With roller, apply charcoal glaze in criss-cross motion over small section of surface (as far as you can reach—you can not walk over wet glaze to complete technique). Glaze, 80/20 mix of glazing liquid and paint thinned with paint thinner, should be transparent enough to see stones through well.

7. Roughly accordion-fold wide plastic strip to crease it, and smooth it down over a stone. Pull off.

8. Immediately dab around edges of stone with a sponge to blend it in and give area in between the texture of cement. Then move on to next stone in section, working fast while glaze is still wet. You can use same strip several times. (Note: Working with a partner can make this easier.) Work section by section, over entire surface. Let dry.

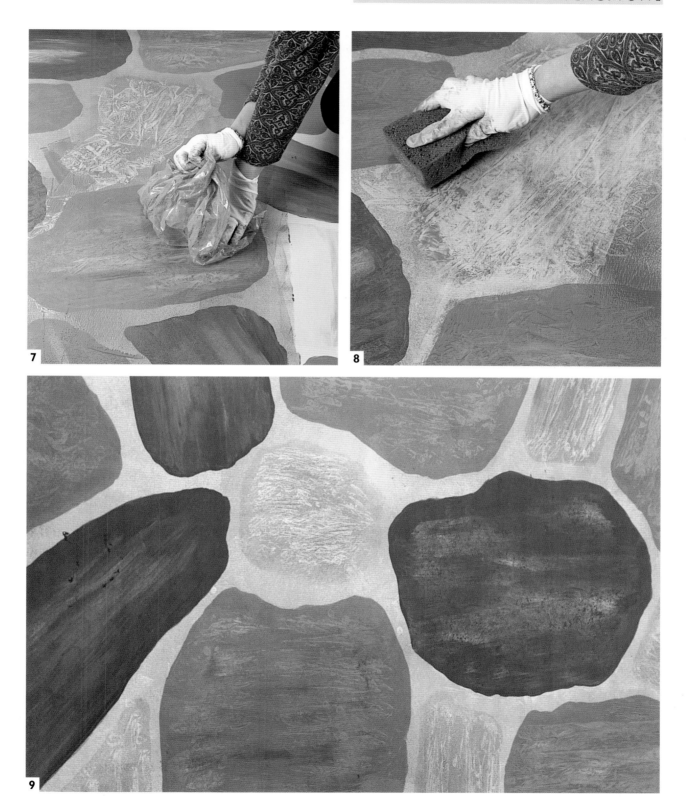

9. Apply several coats of varnish, per instructions on page 95.

<u>RECIPE</u>

FIELDSTONE

LEVEL OF EXPERTISE:

RECOMMENDED ON: Floors, fireplace walls, tub surrounds

NOT RECOMMENDED ON: Highly carved surfaces, small surfaces

NUMBER OF PEOPLE: 2 recommended, but can do with 1

TOOLS: Newspaper or drop cloths; rubber gloves; paint tray; paint roller to apply base coat; newspaper ripped into sizes similar to your stones; 1-inch rounded fitch paint brush; sea sponge; varnishing pad

 BASE COAT: Dove white latex flat interior house paint (or porch, deck, and floor paint)

APPLIED FINISH: 2 oil-based enamel paints

◆ Straw

◆ Ash

VARNISH: Required for floors

One of the many colors and patterns of fieldstone—study the shapes, then do your own freehand version.

With this recipe, it's okay to use just one brush that you don't clean between colors and "contaminate" your paint; allowing the colors to blend together for a slightly dirty effect only adds to the finish.

Like the "Flagstone" and "Granite" finishes in this chapter, and the "Brick" finish in Chapter Nine, faux fieldstone would make great flooring in a sunspace, entry hall, mudroom, or kitchen. If you'll be working on a floor, be sure to first see the notes in the introduction to this chapter on paints to use and what to watch for.

Don't be put off by the thought of painting in the stones freehand. Give your eye something to get a rough idea from, and you'll get them just fine. There's no need to be exact—there are so many colors and patterns of fieldstone; a version like yours exists out there somewhere. And, as when painting the veining in the marbling techniques in Chapter Eight, or the details on the "Grape-Leaf Motif," the best advice is to stay loose. Don't agonize over every paint stroke. Have fun!

Another thing that might surprise you is how you get the "texture" and shading that gives the stones their 3-D look. There's no artistic shading involved; simply press newsprint over the wet glaze, lift off, and there it is. The texture comes from the varying amounts of glaze absorbed by the newsprint.

1. **Over dry base coat, paint in stone shapes with fitch brush and straw paint. Work in sections, painting outline of each stone first, then filling in. Leave roughly the same amount of white space between the stones.**

2. **While paint is still wet, press newspaper over stone shapes and pull off to get textured imprint.**

3. **Paint ash paint over stones, outlining first and then filling in.**

4. **Press newspaper over each stone, then lift off.**

5. **Wet a sea sponge with water, and wring out. Dab sponge in straw paint. Sponge on in between stones, replenishing paint on sponge as needed, to blend edges and soften finish. If finished effect is desired on floor, apply several coats of varnish with paint pad. (See page 95 for varnishing instructions.) Finished effect is featured on opening pages of this chapter.**

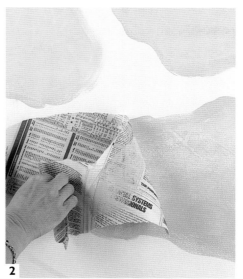

RECIPE

GRANITE

LEVEL OF EXPERTISE:

RECOMMENDED ON: Floors, wall panels, columns

NOT RECOMMENDED ON: Highly carved surfaces

NUMBER OF PEOPLE: 1

TOOLS: Newspapers or drop cloths; rubber gloves; paint roller to apply base coat; paint tray; paint stirrers; graph paper, ruler, and colored pencils or markers to create color diagram of design; pencil; straight edge; level; 1/2-inch masking tape; foam brushes geared to size of project; 3 paint containers; small sea sponge; large sea sponge; paint pad for varnishing

BASE COAT: Dove white latex semi-gloss interior house paint

APPLIED FINISH: 4 latex paint colors

 Taupe

Chalk

 Tawny

 Midnight gray

VARNISH: Use water-based varnish

Knowing how to sponge on can get you far in the world of decorative painting. Here it helps to create a mosaic of inlaid granite that could easily lend a bit of grandeur to an unimposing entry hall. (For more tips on sponging on, turn to the "Marbling" recipes, or the "Stucco" recipe. For a detailed guide to sponging, see the first volume of *Recipes for Surfaces*, page 91.)

You can easily create a pattern like the one you see, which employs a simple checkerboard effect of gray and chalk rectangles, centered by a tawny diamond. Masking tape over the base coat masks out the lines that divide the granite slabs, in much the same way it forms the "mortar" in the "Brick" recipe.

For pattern inspiration, check the floors in both old public buildings and new shopping malls. Granite and its look-alikes are everywhere these days. Colors can be true-to-life or "fantasy."

This finish uses more paint than many of the decorative effects you see in this book. It also employs two sponges instead of the usual one—which, in addition to changing the position of the sponge in your hand frequently, is a good way to get greater variation in your impressions. Here, the larger sponge makes an even overall pattern, while the smaller sponge leaves a more clearly defined "printed" mark.

With stone finishes, varnishing is a big plus because it brings out the depth and color of the effect and gives it a more genuine feel. But, with this particular finish—and any finish that has white areas—be careful which varnish you choose. Whenever you use varnish over white paint, you run the risk of the paint yellowing. Look for a "non-yellowing" formula; but don't take the label at face value. Be sure to test the varnish on a practice surface first.

To begin the technique, apply white base coat with a roller. Let dry. Measure your surface, and then, on graph paper, draw a small color diagram of your granite design to scale (i.e., in proportion to your room).

Sponging lets you replicate the mottled surface of granite, shown above in an inlaid pattern.

1. Reproduce diagram full size, drawing lines lightly over base coat with pencil and straight edge. With level, check that lines are straight. Apply masking tape next to pencil lines, pressing firmly in place to prevent paint seepage. (That way, you'll paint over the pencil lines and won't have to worry about removing them.)

2. With foam brush, apply tawny paint to triangle. Let dry.

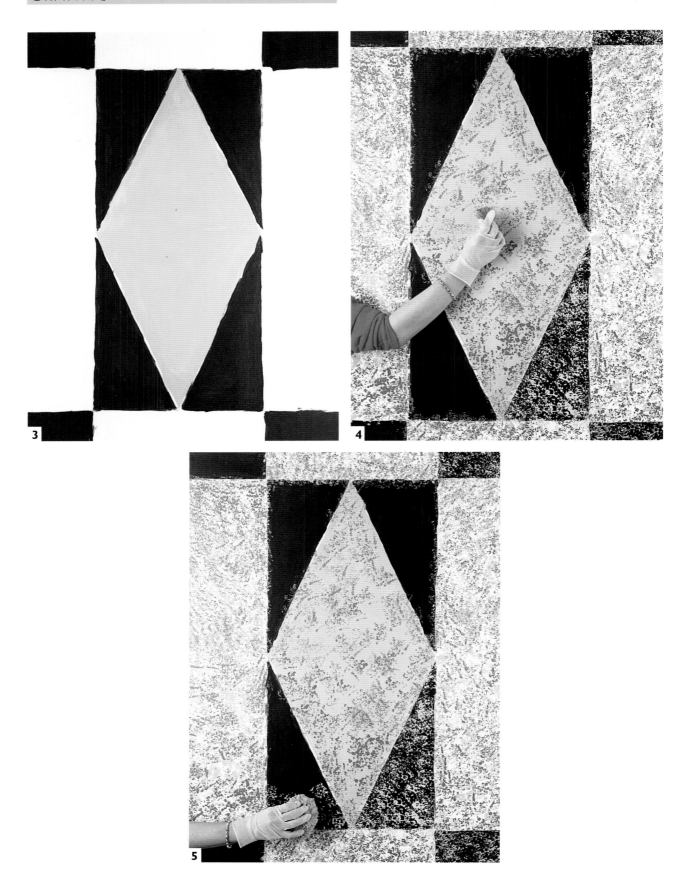

3. With foam brush, apply midnight gray to triangles, adjoining tawny triangle, and to adjacent rectangles in checkerboard fashion. Let dry.

4. Wet sea sponges with water and wring out until damp. Fill containers with tawny, taupe, and midnight gray paint. "Sponge on" over surface. With small sponge, apply taupe paint to entire surface, then tawny paint over white areas only. Paint dries quickly between coats because it's latex and you use so little of it.

5. With large sponge, apply midnight gray paint over entire surface. Let dry.

6. Remove masking tape. Apply two coats of water-based varnish with paint pad. Dip pad into varnish in paint tray. Hold pad flat against surface. Pull pad across surface in single swipes. Don't go back over areas just coated; you'll get any spots you missed with second coat. Let first coat dry before applying second (about 2 to 3 hours).

7. This finish illustrates how much your tools can influence your results. Imprints from two sponges contribute to the look, enhancing the sense of depth.

RECIPE

MALACHITE

LEVEL OF EXPERTISE:

RECOMMENDED ON: Accessories, small surfaces such as tabletops

NOT RECOMMENDED ON: Highly carved surfaces

NUMBER OF PEOPLE: 1

TOOLS: Newspapers or drop cloths; mask; rubber gloves; paint roller or household brush for applying base coat; paint tray; paint thinner; paint stirrers; paper for testing effect on; posterboard, several pieces cut to size of your design's biggest shape; 1/8-inch or 1/4-inch masking tape, depending on project size; 1-inch foam brush; small, flat bristle brush; cotton rags or paper towels; paint pad to apply varnish

 BASE COAT: Clover latex semi-gloss interior house paint

 GLAZE: Oil-based glazing liquid and spruce alkyd low-luster paint

VARNISH: Use water-based varnish

The rich colors and detailed patterns of malachite can be seen in the inlaid edge of this table.

Great expanses of malachite are rare. What you see most often are malachite inlays, like the pattern created here. You can copy or adapt it, or create your own design, depending on the space or object to be painted. You might prefer a simpler design of just squares or rectangles. Or, you might come across an inlay pattern that appeals to you.

Working in smaller sections also makes the technique much easier. In any case, practice will be a big help—you want to feel confident in using your tool and in making the two kinds of marks that characterize malachite: "waves" and "centers."

This recipe employs a version of a decorative painting technique called "dragging." The technique can be challenging when done over great distances—say, from the top to bottom of a wall—but is much easier to master when done in short sections, as seen here. For one thing, if you don't like the way a section comes out, you can just paint over it and drag it again, without interfering with the rest of your design.

For this technique, you'll make your own tool from a piece of posterboard. *Neatly* rip the posterboard into small rectangles the width of the widest shape in your design. How you rip the posterboard is crucial. You don't want to cut it with scissors because you want a feathered edge. But you must tear it very carefully so that you don't get any extra-big gaps in the poster-board that would let too much glaze through and mess up the malachite pattern. Make sure you test each tool you make to be sure you like the impression it creates.

When you drag the wavy sections, start at the top of a shape and decide which way you want the pattern to go. For the "centers," use a small, flat bristle brush and swirl it slightly, pushing it into the glaze so that it forms the lines. Place one center directly adjacent to the next.

Dragging also plays a major part in the recipe for "Sedimentary-Style Marble;" you use the same tool. See page 110 for more tips.

The deep, rich greens of malachite make for an eye-catching finish, but they don't have to limit your color choices. As in the *"Fantasy" Marbling* chapter, you can do this technique in nonconventional colors, as well. However, you may find tone-on-tone combinations most appealing because they offer the least distraction from malachite's distinctive pattern.

This finish looks particularly wonderful on small objects—where you most often see real malachite. To get a sense of the malachite effect small-scale, in 3-D, study the photo of the clock on page 99. (See the section on "Masking," page 68, for tips on preparing the clock for painting.)

1. Measure your surface, then, on graph paper, draw diagram "to scale" (i.e., in proportion to your room) of inlay pattern you want. Then draw full-size pattern on surface, putting in lines lightly over base coat with pencil and straight edge. Check lines with level. Next, apply masking tape lines, pressing firmly to prevent paint seepage.

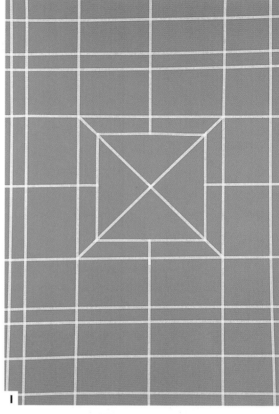

2. With foam brush, blot spruce glaze onto one small inlay section at a time. Paint all the way to edge and over tape.

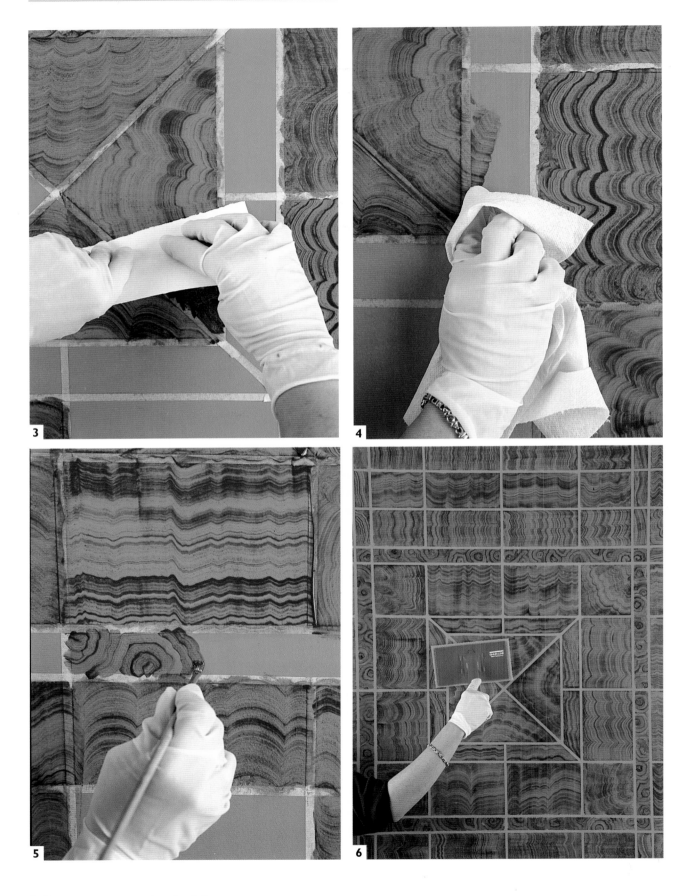

3. Immediately drag posterboard tool over glaze in that section before glaze dries. Use wavy motion, pressing firmly and holding posterboard at 45-degree angle. As you drag, stop briefly after each curve to form natural lines of malachite. Wipe tool on rag before starting next section. Paint and drag every other shape in your design, moving along in the same direction, then let those dry. Vary direction and pattern of your lines, as shown, making some semicircular rows and some bands of wavy lines.

4. Immediately clean up any glaze that runs over into next section with clean, dry cotton rag. Once "non-adjacent" sections have dried, you can tackle the rest of the shapes, one at a time, without smearing the work you've already done.

5. With small, flat bristle brush, paint semi-circular-line pattern in remaining sections.

6. Remove tape. Apply two coats of varnish with small paint pad (See instructions on page 95.)

This simple wood clock was transformed with this recipe for malachite into a one-of-a-kind treasure.

"FANTASY" MARBLING

Marbling is everywhere today—you can find it on everything from sheet sets to photo frames to laminate countertops and vinyl flooring. And, most importantly, you can find it in many more colors than Mother Nature ever intended. Marbling in "fantasy" colors, often accented with metallics, abounds.

In this chapter, you'll find recipes for three imaginative examples—shimmering red, a sparkling blue, and a warm sedimentary-style marble in watercolor hues that conjure up the Grand Canyon at sunset.

Mastering marbling could take a lifetime—but it doesn't have to. So many of the marbleized effects you see today are just impressions of the real thing. Your own interpretation could easily be the best complement to your decorating scheme.

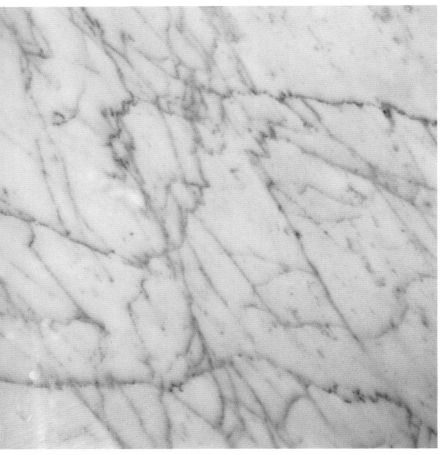

Marble's translucence makes it an ideal subject for the decorative painter—the translucence is replicated by layering paint and glaze. Note, too, the "directional quality" of marble, as seen in the photo above: Veining all runs in the same general direction, like a school of fish.

Note, however, that studying marble and really looking at the shapes that make up this spectacular stone are vital; the more time you put into looking, the more your work will benefit. The more you look, the more you'll see how many kinds of marble there are—travertine, brecciated, variegated, serpentine—and, thus, how many options you have.

Looking carefully will also help you understand the essence and structure of marble. Decorative painting has a crucial quality in common with marble—translucence. Some of marble's veins and coloring show through clearly on the surface; others appear only hazily. This same effect can be achieved by the layering effect of glazes over the base coat.

Marble's layered effect is a result of the way the stone forms: under pressure and through a natural heating and cooling process that forms the veins and fragmented layers, which eventually harden into solid stone.

Something else that will help you get the finish you want is practice. This is no general statement. There is a painterly quality to this technique; you need to experiment with artistic things like "composition," i.e., where you put those light and dark patches, which way you run the veining.

There is, however, a real key to doing this without going to art school: *Think "fish."*

Keeping an open mind, study the photo of real marble at left. Focus on the veining, and you'll see two things: **1)** The lines all flow pretty much in the same direction. Thus, when you do your marbling, choose a main direction to run the veins. **2)** The lines form irregular groups of diamond shapes reminiscent of schools of fish all swimming in the same direction. Keep making rough fish shapes (minus tails, of course), and you'll create a basic structure for your finish that "says" marble.

"Thinking fish" may also help you with another crucial task: Staying loose. Don't go into it thinking, "Marbling is for professionals with years of experience. I've got to concentrate to get it right."

The key is in how you hold your brush when you paint your fish shapes: not like a pencil, but *loosely*, and *by the tip*. The looser you hold it, the more natural your lines will look. And the more lines and layers of color you add, the more you get those feelings of movement and depth, which are the essence of marble.

RECIPE

RED MARBLE

LEVEL OF EXPERTISE:

RECOMMENDED ON: Wall panels, floors, moldings, columns, tabletops, tub surrounds, fireplace mantels, furnishings, accessories

NOT RECOMMENDED ON: Highly carved surfaces

NUMBER OF PEOPLE: 1

TOOLS: Newspaper or drop cloths; mask; rubber gloves; paint tray; paint stirrers; palette; large feathers; paint thinner; 2-inch foam paint brush for raspberry-colored glaze; paint rollers for applying base coat and red glaze; plastic bags or plastic wrap; cotton rags about 12-inches square; paint pad to apply varnish

 BASE COAT: Melon latex semi-gloss interior house paint

 GLAZES: Gold leaf oil-based enamel paint, plus oil-based glazing liquid and 3 alkyd low-luster enamel paints

 Tomato

 Raspberry

 Plum

VARNISH: Use water-based varnish

Although you'll get some seriously beautiful results with this technique, it'll be hard to take the *process* too seriously, considering the tools you use to execute it. What better way to create marble's feathery-edged veining than with a feather? And, instead of struggling with a brush, you can just use scrunched-up plastic bags to mask out those "fish" shapes so characteristic of marble.

For large surfaces, you'll need about five large feathers. You can buy them in fishing-supply stores, and in art supply stores.

Your goal with this finish is to create a sense of depth. To do that, you must break up the surface visually. The gold veining, plus three other glaze colors, overlapped and applied in different manners, help you to do this. To capture the translucence of marble, the three glazes are thinned with enough paint thinner so that the base coat and veining show through, augmenting the layered effect.

Stand back often as you work, and see where you need to darken a light area and vice versa, building up as you go. Always use just a little paint at a time, keeping a light touch and blending the colors. Use darker colors to create shadows around your fish shapes and, thus, give your finish a three-dimensional quality.

There's also a special trick to this finish: varnishing twice—once after painting the veining and once at the end. Why? Damage control. Say you've completed your veining. Now you varnish over it. Then, you put on your next glaze layer, and if you don't like the way it comes out, you can just wipe it off without removing your veining and having to start from scratch.

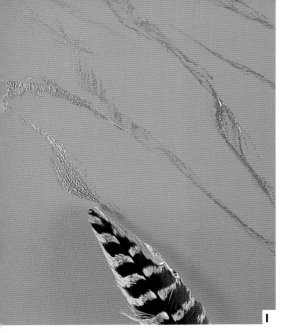

1

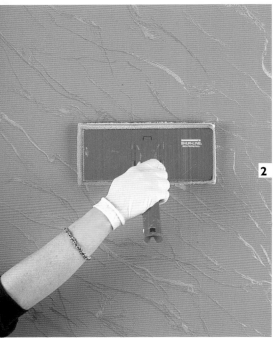

2

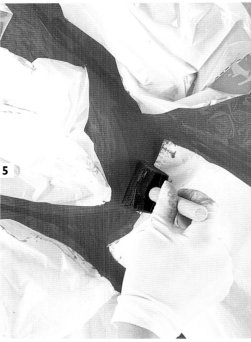

3

1. Pour gold leaf paint into paint tray. Dip top half of feather into paint. Holding feather loosely, run edge and tip downward over base coat, creating pattern of diamonds that looks like fish swimming in same direction. Overlap some "fish," and vary size. Rotate feather slightly by turning wrist as you paint to get thick and thin lines. Let veining dry thoroughly. Set gold paint aside; you'll use it again in step 8. Clean feather with paint thinner, wiping in feather's natural direction.

2. With paint pad, apply varnish over veining. Starting in upper-left corner, swipe pad over surface. For smooth finish, avoid going back over areas already coated. Let dry 24 hours.

3. Pour thin tomato glaze into a paint tray. Apply glaze in criss-cross motion with a roller. Glaze should be transparent enough to see veining and base coat. Set glaze aside; you'll use it again in step 9.

4. Press plastic bags firmly onto wall, shaping them into "fish." Arrange them on diagonal, following fish shapes you created with veining. Overlap some bags. Keep bags from getting square shape. Bags will stick to paint until you remove them. For entire wall, work in 3-foot by 8-foot sections, starting in top corner. (Note: You will need a ladder.)

5. Using raspberry glaze and tip of 2-inch foam brush, paint around plastic bags with loose, rough strokes.

6. Crumple wad of plastic wrap in your hand and dab raspberry glaze to blend it and give soft edge to fish shapes.

4

5

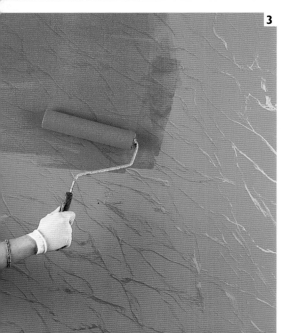

6

7. **Remove plastic bags. Note that some raspberry glaze comes off with bags, leaving light imprints of crumbled plastic. Let glaze dry thoroughly.**

8. **With feather and gold paint, highlight alongside some of the veins. Vary length and placement of highlights—on top, sides, underneath. Follow bolder lines, working to break up surface further. Let dry.**

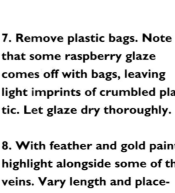

9. **With feather and tomato glaze, darken some areas, following the fish shapes you created. Don't outline the shapes; make V's. Stand back from your work often to see where you need more color. Use a light touch so that you can still see your original gold veins. Let dry.**

10. **With cotton rag, apply plum glaze. (Note: Glaze needn't be as thin as others because it is rubbed on.) Dab rag in glaze, dab off excess on paper— rag should be almost dry. Make streaky lines in same direction as your shapes, in some places roughly outlining shapes for 3-D effect. Apply paint lightly at first and build up, as needed, standing back to see where you can use more color. (If you put on too much paint, just "rag" it off.) Let dry thoroughly.**

11. **For marblelike sheen, apply varnish as in step 2.**

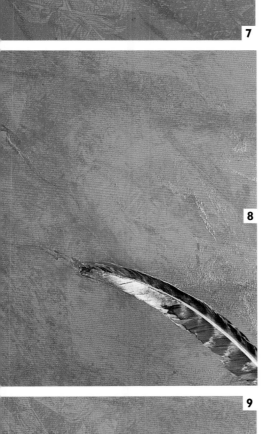

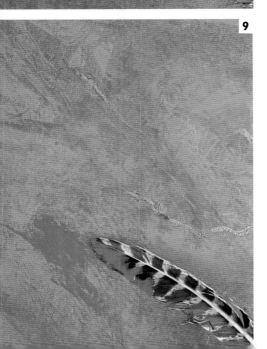

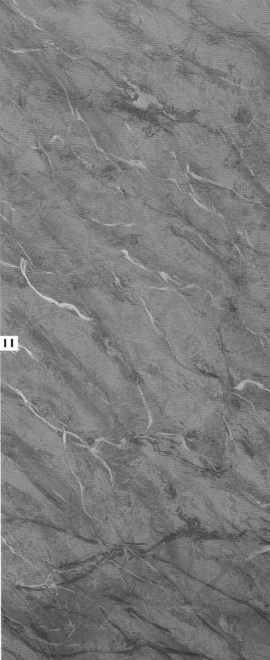

RECIPE

BLUE MARBLE

LEVEL OF EXPERTISE:

RECOMMENDED ON: Wall panels, floors, moldings, columns, tabletops, tub surrounds, fireplace mantels, furnishings, accessories

NUMBER OF PEOPLE: 1

TOOLS: Newspaper or drop cloths; rubber gloves; paint trays; paint stirrers; paint roller for applying base coat; large-size household sponge; sea sponge; palette; paper for testing sponge marks; water for wetting and washing out sponges; silver foil; glue to adhere foil; feather to smooth glue; paint pad to apply varnish

BASE COAT: Powder-blue latex semi-gloss interior paint

APPLIED FINISH: 4 latex interior paint colors, plus silver foil for veining

 Sail blue

 Caribbean green

 Dark teal

 Salmon

VARNISH: Use water-based varnish

Colors from an Impressionist painting, just a hint of silver veining . . . this fantasy marble could easily liven up a room or give a worn old object new life.

And it's simple to do. That's because it relies mainly on one of the most easily mastered decorative painting techniques—sponging on, which involves "printing" multiple layers of sponged impressions over your base coat. It's these multiple layers that give the finish the sense of depth you get when you look at genuine marble.

You'll use two kinds of sponges to get extra variation in the impressions you make—

household and sea sponge. The household sponge puts in a background pattern (over your base coat). Any size will do, but the larger sizes are easier to hold. Also, with the range of sponges available in your local store today, be sure to get the old-fashioned kind with small holes, not a "scrub-brush" type—the pattern will be too distinctive.

The sea sponge helps you add depth, by creating softer layers and blending your colors slightly. Because of the popularity of decorative painting, sea sponges are more readily available than ever. You can get them in craft and paint stores now, as well as in drug and cosmetic shops.

Because you're using latex paints, you can buy just one of each kind of sponge and wash them out between colors. Before you begin, however, you'll want to cut the edges off your sponges so that they have a more rounded, fishlike shape (more like the shapes you find in real marble).

Remember that a major distinctive feature of marble is its directional flow. In the previous recipe, for "Red Marble," you created fishlike shapes "swimming" *on the diagonal.* For this particular recipe, you want those same "fish" to swim *vertically.* Any imprints you put on your surface should be in the vertical direction.

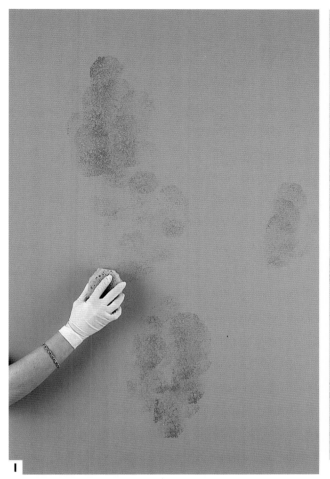

1

2

1. Put sail blue paint on palette. Wet household sponge, and dip in glaze. Test sponge on paper, dabbing off excess. Starting at top of wall, dab sponge lightly in random groupings.

2. Create "schools of fish" swimming in vertical direction. Overlap some "fish." Use only a little paint so that texture of sponge is visible.

HOW TO GET THOSE SPARKLING SILVER VEINS

What really makes this marble sparkle is its silver veining. You can create it easily with commercially available products—silver foil, which comes prepackaged in sheets, and glue for the foil, which comes in a small squeeze bottle. Both are usually available in craft and fabric stores (they're used for decorating T-shirts); be sure to follow the application and drying instructions for your particular brand. If you can't find them in your area, you can use silver paint. Apply it with a feather in the same manner as the gold paint in the previous recipe. The feather will also come in handy when applying the glue. Use it to "feather out" the edges of the glue line you "draw on," giving your veining a more natural look.

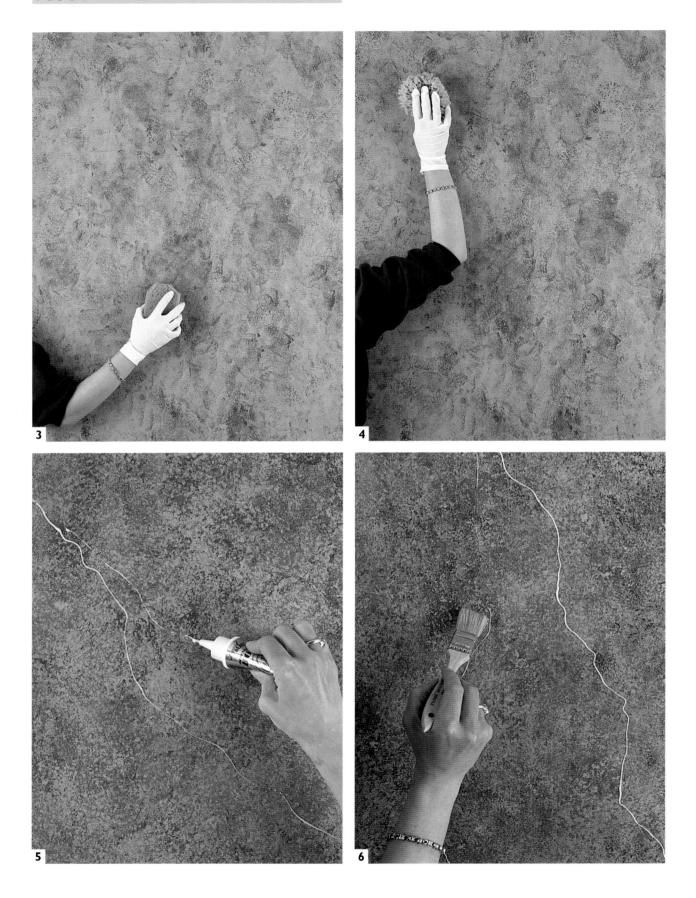

3. Repeat step 1 using Caribbean green paint and filling in between sail blue sponged impressions. Paint dries quickly, so you don't have to wait long before applying next layer. Repeat step 1 again, using dark teal paint. Overlap sail blue and Caribbean green impressions and fill in around edges.

4. Switch to sea sponge. Wet it first, then repeat Step 1, using salmon paint. Go over most of surface, blending colors and adding depth. Then with wet sea sponge, apply random impressions of three other paints (sail blue, Caribbean green, and dark teal). Rinse out sponge and let surface dry approximately ten minutes between each color.

5. Let surface dry completely. Then, starting at top of wall, apply glue in shape of veining. Squeeze out a thin layer, holding your wrist loosely so that you can make squiggly lines. (If you get glue where you don't want it, wash it off immediately; it won't come off once dry.)

6. With feather or small, soft brush, "feather out" edges of glue to create fade-away effect. Let glue dry, overnight if required, until it is opaque and tacky.

7. Press sheet of silver foil over part of glue, rub thumb over veining, and lift sheet off. (Foil will remain on surface.) Repeat process until all glue is covered with foil.

8. With paint pad, varnish surface in smooth, sweeping strokes. (See page 31 for varnishing tips.) Look of finished effect will vary, depending on light in which it is seen.

RECIPE

SEDIMENTARY-STYLE MARBLE

LEVEL OF EXPERTISE:

RECOMMENDED ON: Walls, wall panels, columns, tabletops, tub surrounds, furnishings, accessories

NUMBER OF PEOPLE: 2 recommended, depending on project size

TOOLS: Newspaper or drop cloths; mask; rubber gloves; paint tray; paint roller for applying base coat; paint stirrers; plastic cups to hold paint; paint thinner; 2-inch household bristle brush; 1-inch foam bristle brush; No. 5 sable brush; paper for testing tools on; 3-inch by 5-inch cardboard pieces for "dragging" paint; paper towels; cotton rags for touch-up; paint-scraping pad for splattering paint; paint pad to apply varnish

◆ BASE COAT: Dove white latex semi-gloss interior house paint

GLAZES: Oil-based glazing liquid and 5 alkyd low-lustre paint colors

◆ Saddle

◆ Turquoise

◆ Eggplant

◆ Clay

◆ Buff

VARNISH: Use water-based varnish

If Santa Fe is your decorating style of choice, this finish may be just what you've been looking for. A great alternative to overstylized wallpaper options of the Santa Fe genre, it evokes the type of stone you find at the Grand Canyon.

In the watercolorlike hues shown here, the finish is a real attention-getter. But, by using several shades of a neutral hue, you can easily "turn down" the color intensity to "desert at daybreak." A beautiful tone-on-tone version could turn a room into the perfect showcase for a collection of Santa Fe furnishings, fabrics, and artifacts.

To do a whole room, you'll benefit from working with a partner. You'll need to paint in long strips across the room, and it will be helpful to have someone to move your ladder as you go. Or, you may find it easier to set up scaffolding so that you can move easily across your wall without having to walk up and down.

Practice is especially important with this finish. It is based on a traditional decorative painting technique used by wood grainers. Called "dragging," it can take a little time to master because it requires a somewhat steady hand. (You can find a detailed guide to dragging—as well as other dragged finishes you might like to try once you've mastered the technique—beginning on page 180 of the first volume of *Recipes for Surfaces*.) Dragging can be done with a wide range of tools—combs, paint brushes, even steel wool. For this finish, the paint is dragged with a piece of cardboard.

A small detail that will make a big difference with this technique: how you get your cardboard to the size you need. Don't cut it with a scissors. Rip it, to get a feathered edge. But rip it neatly—you don't want any big gaps in the edge because too much paint might pass through them and distort the effect. Be sure you test your piece of cardboard before using it on your wall to make sure it creates a pleasing pattern.

1. With 1-inch foam brush, paint on horizontal stripes of saddle glaze. Hold brush flat against wall, varying pressure as you go across surface to create dark and light spots. Lines should be wavy, even streaky. Be sure to leave some white space between lines.

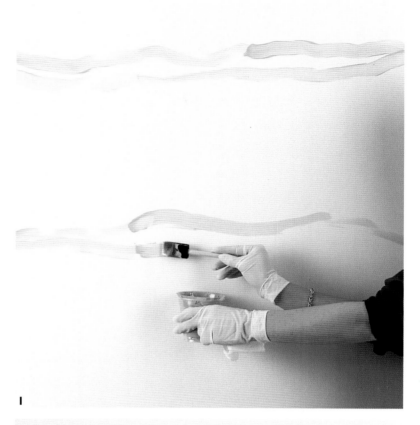

2. Immediately after you paint lines, "drag" over them with a 3-inch by 5-inch piece of cardboard (that you have carefully ripped, not cut with scissors). Wiggle cardboard as you drag it across. Wipe cardboard on paper towel after each pass. Replace cardboard when it gets saturated. Let glaze dry.

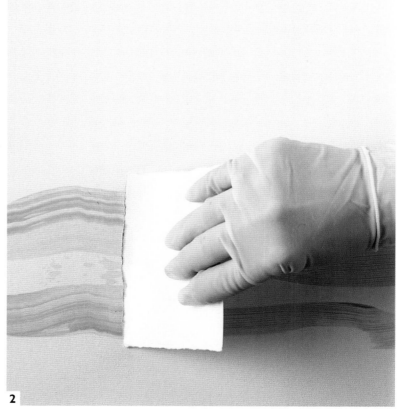

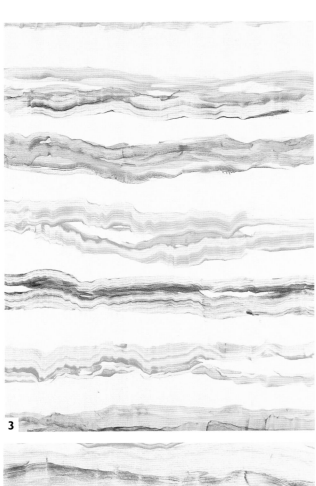

"FANTASY" MARBLING

3. Repeat process with eggplant glaze, putting in eggplant stripes between saddle stripes. Let glaze dry.

4. Paint on water streaks of buff glaze, filling in between saddle and eggplant stripes. Drag over buff glaze with dry 2-inch household bristle brush. Let glaze dry. Paint on turquoise glaze. Use it as an accent— paint in between every few stripes, over buff glaze in spots. If it gets too dark, wipe off with cotton rag.

5. With clay glaze and No. 5 sable brush, add in brush strokes to bring out some veining. Hold brush by tip, and roll it, to make wavy, wiggly lines. Don't hold brush like a pencil—the looser you hold it, the more natural lines will look. Add more veining with brush and turquoise glaze, then with buff glaze. The more lines and layers of color you add, the more you get a feeling of depth.

6. Pour some eggplant glaze in paint tray. Dip in paint-scraping pad, and "off-load" excess glaze on paper. Dab pad randomly over surface. (Note: This is the "Spattering" technique. For a detailed guide, see page 148.) Fill in with spots in areas where surface is least busy.

7. With a paint pad, varnish surface for marblelike sheen. See page 95 for instructions.

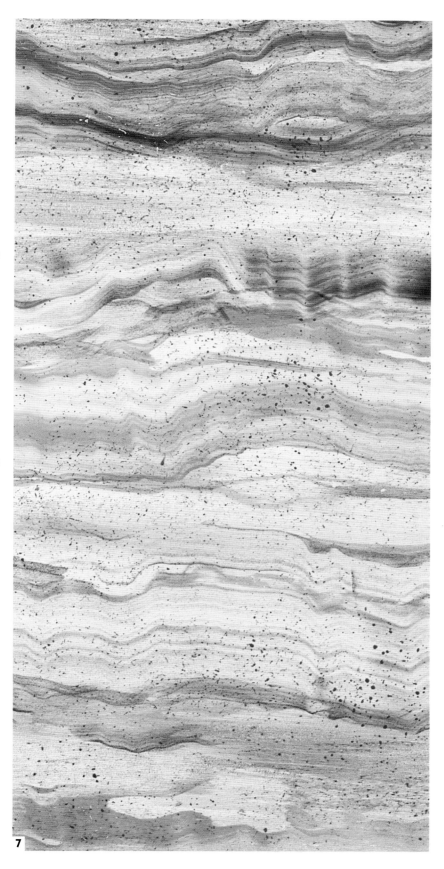

7

CHAPTER NINE

REASONABLE REPLICAS

You can go to school for years to learn how to reproduce some of the materials featured in this chapter. Or, you can get these attractive, fun, and easily attainable versions by following the simple recipes found here.

With these finishes, you have the opportunity to get a classic or "decorator" look at a fraction of the cost. The warmth and depth of frescoed walls can be yours without the plaster and pains-taking execution, thanks to a technique as simple as polishing shoes. A country kitchen with a real brick floor may be a dream based on something you saw in a magazine; but you can capture some of the rusticity with the brick finish that is included in this chapter, using the easily mastered technique of sponging.

Decorative painting lets you capture a late-afternoon cloudy sky, shown here embellished with grape-vine motifs in a designer-show-house room.

If you've always wanted fabric-covered walls, take a look at the recipe for "Moire," reminiscent of a beautiful blue Chinese water silk. (The same simple graining technique lets you mimic wood paneling.) And what could be more classic, or more refreshing on a dark day, than a cloud ceiling—one that, instead of painting, you rub on with a cloth.

Before starting on any of these recipes, take some time to study the materials you plan to reproduce. There's no need to copy them exactly. What you're striving for is the general look and feel. For example,

how do the natural creases in leather fall? How do clouds *really* look? It's when you can transfer the unique characteristics of a material to your painted finish that it really takes on life. To get you started, we've included photographs of the materials. But take your research further. That's what artists do, and it pays off.

Once you're ready to begin, a positive, can-do attitude will be your best friend. Don't be intimidated by how difficult you've *heard* it is to do a finish. The best way to gain confidence is to practice on some sample boards first.

RECIPE

FRESCO

LEVEL OF EXPERTISE:

RECOMMENDED ON:
Walls

NUMBER OF PEOPLE: 1

TOOLS: Newspapers or drop cloths; paint tray; paint stirrers; paint thinner; mask; rubber gloves; paint roller to apply base coat; cotton sheeting, cut into squares about 12 inches

BASE COAT:
Linen white latex semi-gloss interior housepaint

 GLAZE: Oil-based glazing liquid and pumpkin alkyd low-lustre paint

VARNISH: Optional

Nancy and Jeffrey Brooks, the interior designers of the show-house room (shown *opposite*), assisted Nick Devlin, the muralist, by stenciling in individual leaf shapes for the background of the grapevine.

When it comes to giving a room the soft, warm glow you see in venerable old homes and the pages of magazines, few finishes do more than fresco. An ancient technique associated with mural painting and having its roots in Italy, fresco involves applying pigment to still-wet plaster.

Instead of struggling with plaster and trowel, however, you can get some of the same depth of color and subtle textured look with paint. This is a great technique for beginners. There are no complicated brush strokes to learn—in fact, it's as simple as polishing furniture.

Using an easy motion, you make small circles all over your surface, then blend the edges of the circles into one another. Where the circles overlap, you get the lights and darks that give the finish great depth.

Two keys to this technique: Use only a little glaze on your rag at a time, and make sure your rag is lint-free and that the ends of the rag stay tucked in (gathered up into your palm) at all times.

You may be surprised at how dark you have to tint your glaze just to get the subtle color you see here—and at how dark the glaze is when you first dab it on the wall. But it makes sense when you think of all the rubbing you'll do.

The best advice is, if you want your glaze to be the color of the lightest chip in the row on a paint chart, tint it until it is the color of the darkest chip in that row. Otherwise, you're sure to be disappointed because the more you rub the finish, the more paint you remove and, thus, the lighter it will be.

Because you're working with oil-based glaze, you'll have plenty of time to blend your circles well before the edges dry. But do keep in mind that this technique is a "one-shot deal": Once it's dry, it can't be changed. You need to step back from your work periodically to see the light-and-dark effects you're creating. And you must work in sections. If you have to stop, do it at an inconspicuous place: i.e., over a doorway or before starting the next wall.

1. Fold your rag up into your hand so that all the ends are tucked in. Dab a little pumpkin glaze on your rag. Rub the glaze onto the wall with a circular motion. Then, working in sections about 3 feet by 3 feet, randomly select spots within the section you're working on, and rub on more circles.

2. Blend the edges of one circle into the next. Dip your rag into the glaze again, taking care to pick up just a little, and repeat process, section by section.

3. A close-up of the finished effect reveals its subtle texture and depth of color.

RECIPE

LEATHER

LEVEL OF EXPERTISE:

RECOMMENDED ON: Walls

NUMBER OF PEOPLE: 2 recommended, but 1 can do

TOOLS: Newspapers or drop cloths; rags; rollers to apply base coat and glaze; paint trays; paint stirrers; paint thinner; mask; rubber gloves; scissors; plastic dry-cleaner bags or super-lightweight plastic sheeting (1 mm), enough to cover your entire surface

 BASE COAT: Barn red latex semi-gloss interior house paint

 GLAZE: Oil-based glazing liquid and garnet alkyd low-luster paint

VARNISH: Optional

Leather is taking home furnishings by storm these days—but we're not talking about the "library look," with matching burgundy tufted chairs, or a midnight assault of Harley-Davidson black. Leather now often appears in concert with other fabrics and textures—for instance, a leather sofa sporting canvas pillows might be paired with denim-upholstered armchairs and leather toss pillows.

Colorwise, you can hardly go wrong by sticking with the deep, rich hues of the "fine Corinthian leather" shown here; it can lend warmth to any setting. But consider that today you have a lot more freedom—and a lot more sources of inspiration. Real leather comes in more colors than ever, from the most traditional hunter green to shocking pink, baby blue, and royal purple. What might work in your rooms?

If the leather look is for you, you'll need to do a bit of advanced planning: Start saving those bags your clothes come home from the dry cleaners in. In fact, if you plan to do a whole room, ask your family and friends to save theirs, too. You'll need enough bags to cover your entire surface because the bags get full of paint and are tough to reuse.

Getting the leather look is easier than you think. You roll on glaze over your base coat, slap on the bags one next to the other, smooth them out to create the "crevices" you find in leather, then pull them off. Because you're using oil-based glaze—and covering it with plastic—you have plenty of time to get those "crevices" just the way you want them before the paint dries. And the bags won't fall off the walls as you work; they stick to the paint until you're ready to take them down.

The technique is more easily done by two—it's helpful to have someone assist you in putting up the plastic. But one person can definitely do it on her own, as you see here.

Note that with the leather finish, you want the "crevices" to run in many directions, just as they do on the real thing. (For a similar, but more "directional" look, see "Plastic-Wrap Ragging Off.") This is what gives the finish its character. To get this, you can just smooth out the bags and let them go however they go, or you can step back and decide how to arrange them to your liking.

Before you begin, mask off everything in the room you don't want to get glaze on (i.e., ceiling, door jambs, wood moldings, windows). Then, turn dry-cleaner bags into painting tools: With a pair of scissors, cut the edges off the bags, and open the sides.

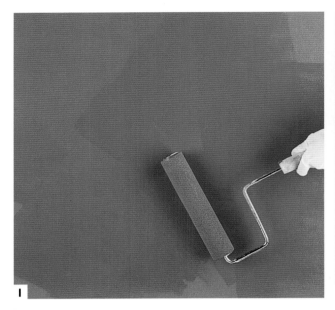

1. Over dry base coat, apply glaze with roller. Then immediately begin putting bags over wet glaze, working with a partner, if possible, to make the process easier. Do one entire wall at a time. Be sure you have enough plastic to cover entire surface.

2. Smooth bags, forming "crevices" that create leather look.

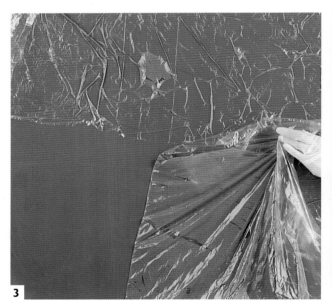

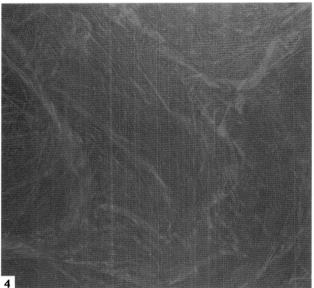

3. Once "smoothing" is complete, pull all bags off at once.

4. A view of the leather-look finish shows creases across the surface in many directions.

Here's a very liveable, and increasingly popular, color combination you might not have considered before—maize and ash. The maize brightens a room, while the ash keeps it well within the range of easy-to-live-with neutrals.

In this recipe, combining yellows and grays also gives you an appealing approximation of stucco. And you can take it a step further: Pair the finish with the "Fieldstone" on page 90 for a pleasing rendition of an old stone wall. The stucco is the background, while the stones fill in here and there, as if the stucco has crumbled and chipped away in spots.

You'll be pleased at how easy it is to master the technique that gives you this sophisticated effect. Sponging on—in which you use a sea sponge to apply glazes to your surface—gives you the subtle texture of stucco.

You can find sea sponges in paint, craft, and home stores, as well as drug and cosmetic shops these days. Work with a piece of sponge cut to the size of your hand so that it's comfortable for you. (For more tips on sponging, read the recipes for "Marbling." For a detailed guide to sponging refer to the first volume of *Recipes for Surfaces*, Chapter Five.)

The colors in stucco are the same as those in the recipe for "Stone;" but here they are softened by the addition of white.

RECIPE

STUCCO

LEVEL OF EXPERTISE:

RECOMMENDED ON:
Walls, ceilings

NUMBER OF PEOPLE: 1

TOOLS: Newspapers or drop cloths; paint tray; paint stirrers; roller to apply base coat; mask; rubber gloves; sea sponge; paper for testing sponge

BASE COAT:
Dove white latex flat interior house paint

GLAZES: Watered-down latex paint (20 percent paint, 80 percent water)

 Light maize

Light ash

VARNISH: No (sheen would detract from look)

The glazes are made of latex paint, watered down to a watercolorlike quality. (The mix that gives you this subtle wash of color is about 20 percent paint, 80 percent water.)

Be sure to mix enough of each glaze for the entire project so that your colors are consistent throughout. Another color-consistency tip: Stir glazes often as you work. The reason for this is that when you first dip your sponge into a glaze, you pick up more water than paint and, over time, the paint settles to the bottom. You may need to add a bit more water as you go through your projects.

The key to this technique is working layer by layer. You always need to be aware of how much paint is on your sponge. This is a building-up process—and it can happen much quicker than you think. It's easy to get too much paint on your surface. You don't want the finish to be too bright. You want a soft, natural look—a cloudy finish with a lot of depth. This is where your "designer's eye" comes in and where it's advantageous to work in thin layers: You get more time to see how the finish is building up. Have patience—you can always add more paint, but once you get a dark spot, you're in trouble because your eye will aways go to that spot. You might end up having to balance the spot with another or make the whole room darker.

Well-worn and weathered stucco features an appealing mix of soft, almost neutral hues.

1. Pour light maize paint into tray. Wet sponge with water. Mix paint and water in paint tray to a very watery consistency. Keep a rag handy in case you have to clean up any drips. Dip sponge into paint and water mixture and wring out. Blot on newspaper to remove excess paint and to check the impression being made by the sponge.

2. Bunch sponge up in your hand, holding it straight. Pat sponge lightly to surface working in a 4-foot section. Vary the direction of the sponge by shifting your wrist when the sponge is in the air. Move your pats to concentrate in different areas and fill in between the heaviest spots as the paint diminishes on the sponge. Work until the sponge is almost dry. Before you repeat the sponging, step back and examine the distribution of the paint on the surface to see if the light and dark marks are pleasingly balanced.

3. Re-dip sponge in glaze and unload most of the color before you repeat step 2. Always test your sponge before applying it to the wall, to make sure you have the color you want. Step back from your project as you work to insure you're "making waves," that is, creating lighter and darker patches of color. Repeat the process with light ash color. Starting with light impressions and building up color intensity through layering.

4. A close-up of this delicate finish discloses the pleasing mix of light maize and light ash that "says" stucco.

3

4

RECIPE

CLOUDY SKY

LEVEL OF EXPERTISE:

RECOMMENDED ON: Ceilings

NUMBER OF PEOPLE: 1

TOOLS: Newspaper or drop cloths; mask; rubber gloves; paint tray; paint roller for applying base coat; paint thinner; paint stirrers; 12-inch square cotton rags

BASE COAT: Sky blue latex flat interior house paint

APPLIED FINISH: White oil-based enamel paint

VARNISH: No

What better way to transform a boxy room than by opening it to the outdoors? If breaking through the walls or the roof just aren't options, you can use this recipe to bring the "wild blue yonder" inside.

Before you begin, spend some time looking up. Study the sky under a variety of weather conditions and times of day, and sketch or photograph cloud patterns you like.

Keep in mind, however, that puffy clouds can be tougher to paint than wispy ones. The wispy clouds created with this recipe are easier to master and still give a satisfying effect.

The most likely place you'll want to execute this finish is on the ceiling; so give some thought now to how you'll paint up there. Artists usually try to set up a moveable platform called scaffolding, which you can either rent or build yourself. The scaffolding should be high enough to bring you within comfortable arm's reach of the ceiling either when you're lying on your back or kneeling, whichever way you're more comfortable painting.

This recipe employs three ways of using a cotton rag: dragging, pulling, and ragging-on with it. Working with a rag instead of a brush will probably be a blessing for the beginning painter. You're less likely to end up with a stereotypical notion of what clouds should look like with this less-traditional painting tool. Be sure to prepare your rags carefully before you start. They need to be lint free so that you don't end up with any foreign particles in your painted finish. Cut your cloth with a scissors or pinking shears to prevent fraying; you may want to machine wash and dry it, then run a lint brush or masking tape over it to remove fuzz.

You'll find additional instructions for the ragging-on technique under the "Corduroy Ragging On." (For a detailed guide to ragging, see first volume of *Recipes for Surfaces*, page 110.)

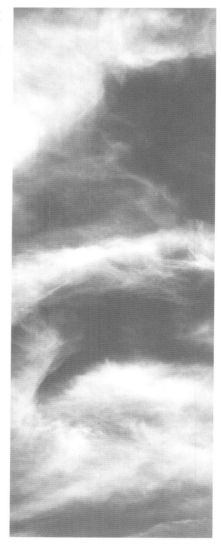

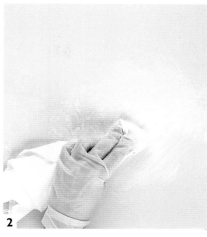

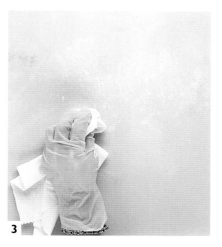

1

2

3

1. Fold rag to form long, flat "printing surface." Dip rag into paint, then blot off on paper until almost dry. Working in sections, apply with soft, curved sweeping strokes.

2. While paint is still wet, pull rag through sweeps of white paint to create hazy effect.

3. Crumple rag in hand, and dip in paint. Off-load excess until rag is almost dry. "Rag on" over surface to further soften effect and enhance airy, cloudlike feel. Touch rag to surface lightly, turning wrist when rag is in air to vary impressions. Dab wall in spots randomly so that impressions made when rag has most paint on it are scattered throughout.

4

4. Cloudy sky at 10 a.m. Or, change the colors and get a late-afternoon look, as in the photo of the designer-show-house room, page 116.

RECIPE

BRICK

LEVEL OF EXPERTISE:

RECOMMENDED ON: Walls, floors

NOT RECOMMENDED ON: Highly carved surfaces, small objects

NUMBER OF PEOPLE: 1

TOOLS: Newspaper or drop cloths; mask; rubber gloves; paint trays; paint roller; paint thinner; piece of cardboard, about 8 inches by 10 inches; craft knife; a brick (optional — to trace size of and examine colors of); light-tack masking tape; plastic spoon to press down tape lines; foam brush (geared to size of job); sea sponge; paper for testing sponge imprint; varnishing pad

BASE COAT: Latex semi-gloss interior house paint—2 paint colors: Paint on first color, mortar, let dry, then tape over to mask out mortar, and apply second color, melon.

 Mortar

 Melon

APPLIED FINISH: 3 oil-based enamel paint colors

 Terra Cotta

 Brown

 Black

VARNISH: Required for floors

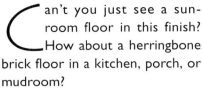

Can't you just see a sunroom floor in this finish? How about a herringbone brick floor in a kitchen, porch, or mudroom?

The simple decorative-painting techniques of "sponging on" give you the ruddy-red bricks, while the color in between is simply a mortar base coat, kept glaze-free during the sponging process with masking tape.

For wood floors in poor condition, paint can be an ideal remedy. You need to prepare them properly, by repairing, stripping, sanding, and priming them, as needed. (For a guide to surface preparation, see Chapter Three.)

Highly durable porch and deck paint is most likely your best choice for the base coat, topped by oil-based glazes. You'll also want to apply several coats of varnish made for flooring to protect your design. Try to get varnish with a flat finish; too much shine on the surface might spoil the effect.

Keep in mind, too, that with floors you must plan to "paint yourself out of the room." You'll end up starting over if you walk over your finish before it dries.

In creating a herringbone pattern, you apply tape lines on a diagonal to form an angled grid. The space between lines should be the width of one brick. The best way to set the width is to trace an actual brick on cardboard twice, cut out the two shapes, and use them to mark the space between lines. You also need to determine the pitch of your diagonal lines and the angle

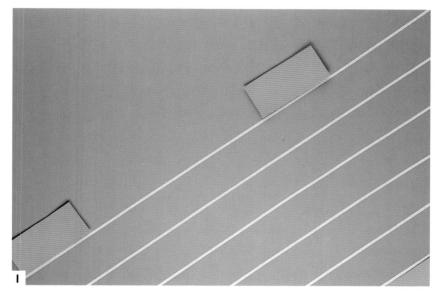

1

2

1. Cut out two cardboard rectangles the size of bricks. (To get size right, trace actual brick.) Put up diagonal tape guidelines in one direction across surface. Lines should be width of one brick apart; use cardboard-cutout bricks to measure off spaces.

2. Apply tape guidelines on diagonal in opposite direction— again, width of one brick apart—so tape forms angled grid on surface.

their intersections should form. Find a few examples of brick herringbone, actual or in photos, including the one on the previous page; take your cue from them.

One challenge with this recipe: Cutting out the correct pieces of tape from your initial grid to form the herringbone pattern. This can be tricky, so go slow. Stop often to check you're removing the right sections. If you make a mistake, just replace the tape and press it firmly back in place.

Colorwise, if classic red is too overpowering for your scheme, light pink, pale yellow, soft beige, white, or even a "fantasy" color can work. But if you feel the effect of a whole wall would be too heavy-looking for your interior, consider interspersing a few bricks over a neutral background instead—as if the bricks were just visible where the plaster of an old wall had chipped away.

To begin, apply mortar base coat with roller. Let dry overnight.

3. Press all tape lines firmly in place with back of a spoon or a credit card to prevent seepage. With craft knife, starting in one corner of surface, cut out parts of tape lines to form herringbone pattern. This can be tricky, so go slow. Stop often to make sure you're removing right part of tape lines. If you make a mistake, just replace tape and press firmly back in place.

4. Using foam brush, paint over entire surface with melon paint in uneven, criss-crossing strokes to begin creating "rough" brick surface. Let dry.

5. Dip sea sponge into paint thinner, and wring well. Pour terra cotta glaze color into paint tray. Dab sponge into paint, then blot off and test impression on paper. "Sponge on" over entire surface: Repeatedly touch sponge lightly to wall, twisting your wrist or arm when sponge is off surface to vary impression. After dipping sponge in terra cotta, don't make marks all in one small area or you'll get a dark spot; touch surface randomly to distribute evenly when sponge has most glaze on it.

6. Repeat step 5 with black glaze.

7. Repeat step 5 with brown glaze. Apply black more sparingly, however, so that finish doesn't get too dark.

8. Remove tape guidelines. Varnish surface, following instructions on page 95.

9. The finished product.

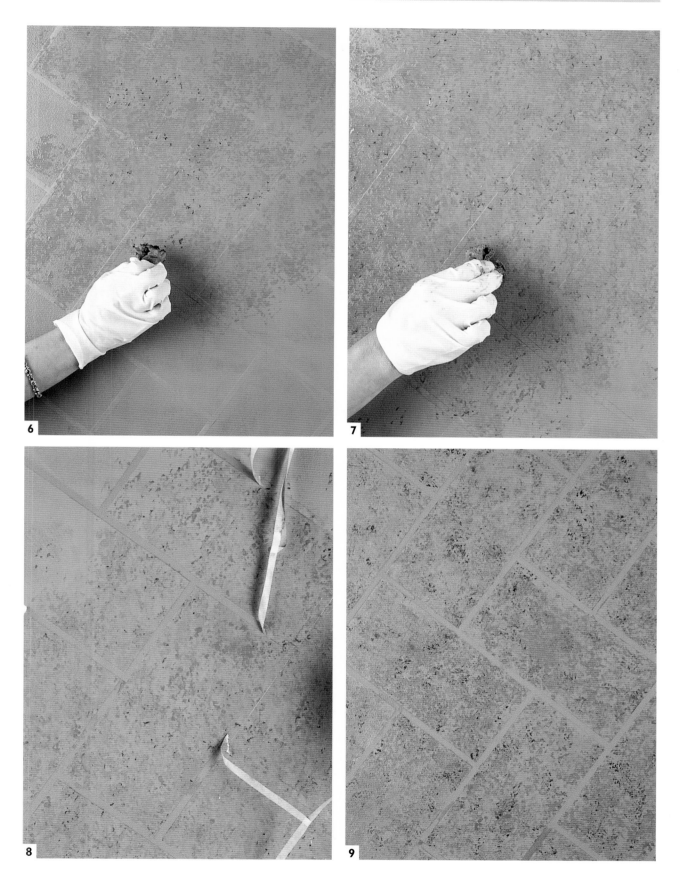

RECIPE

MOIRE

LEVEL OF EXPERTISE:

RECOMMENDED ON: Flat, even surfaces—walls, including below chair rail as faux wainscotting, tabletops, furniture

NOT RECOMMENDED ON: Highly carved surfaces, small objects

NUMBER OF PEOPLE: 2 recommended, especially for large jobs requiring a ladder

TOOLS: Newspaper or drop cloths; mask; rubber gloves; paint roller for applying base coat; paint tray; paint stirrers; 2-inch light-tack masking tape; chalk pencil (or regular pencil); level; foam paint brush; paint container; #10 heart-graining tool; graining comb; cheesecloth, cut into small squares

BASE COAT: Light blue latex interior house paint

GLAZE: Oil-based glazing liquid and sapphire alkyd low-luster paint

VARNISH: Optional

Just the mention of "graining" may be enough to make those familiar with decorative painting hesitate. Certainly, realistically reproducing wood grains might take years of practice, but there is plenty of room in between for creating attractive effects with the same tools.

That being said, however, keep in mind that practice and a steady, experienced hand will still be your best help with this recipe.

The tools you use to create the look of that satiny, water-marked fabric called moire are the same as the wood grainer's: a heart grainer (#10 size) and a graining comb. The tools are available in paint and art supply stores. The combs come in a package with several sizes. For your project, choose a comb that makes an imprint similar to the pattern your graining tool makes; similar width of the tools' "teeth" is what you should be looking at in making your choice. If you can't find a comb that's similar, all isn't lost; the difference will just make the strips stand out more from one another than you see here.

Another way to get an overall similarity to your finish is to count as you work. This method of monitoring your work without agonizing over it can be used with many of the techniques. In this case, it means that when you start graining over a strip of wet glaze, you count the number of squiggles you make and then generally repeat that same amount in subsequent strips. You don't want each row to be the same, but if you look at rows of wood paneling, you can see there is a relationship between the proportion of the grains from one panel to another. That's the kind of similarity you want.

Note that the shorter the distance you do your graining over, the easier the technique will be for you. A great place to do it is below a chair rail in place of wainscotting.

If you are doing it over a whole wall, you'll need a partner—one person to apply the glaze, and another to do the graining before the glaze dries. Don't switch jobs midway through the project. The way each person does decorative painting is as personal as his or her signature—a switch to a lighter touch or a wavier graining line will stand out and distract from the overall effect.

Note, too, that for a whole wall, you'll be working with a ladder, which can be tricky to get on and off of while keeping your hand steady. You'll need that second person to move the ladder for you and vice versa.

Whatever happens, don't lift your graining tool off the wall in mid-strip. The spot where you stopped will be extremely noticeable. If you must stop, you'll need to repaint the strip and start graining again.

1. Over dry base coat, apply vertical strips of light-tack masking tape to wall to mask out strips to be painted first. Make space between strips of masking tape as wide as your graining tool. In this case, the tool used was 3 inches wide; so tape was applied every 3 inches. Mark wall with chalk pencil to indicate where each strip goes. (Note that you can adjust the width of the "in-between" strips slightly so that you end up with the right amount of space in corners of a room.)

2. As you move across your surface, use a level to check that strips are straight.

3. With foam brush or small roller, paint glaze over first untaped strip of wall. Start at bottom and stroke on glaze from side to side.

5. Wrap piece of cheese-cloth on end of your finger and dab out any drips. Then move on to rest of wall, repeating steps 3, 4, and 5. Wipe graining tool off on cloth between passes. When all the untaped strips have been painted, take down tape and let dry overnight.

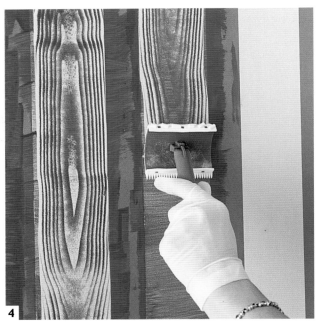

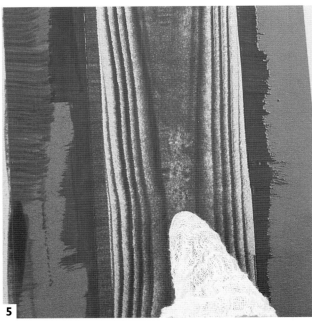

4. Immediately after painting strip, while glaze is still wet, go over strip with graining tool, starting at top of strip and rocking tool from side to side to get effect. Let tape be your guide as you rock tool. Do not lift tool off wall while moving down strip. (If you do, you'll need to repaint strip and start over.)

6. With foam brush, apply glaze to first of remaining strips to be painted, running brush down strip in short vertical strokes.

7. While glaze is still wet, go over strip with graining comb. **Wiggle tool as you move down wall to get wavy lines.** Keep strip as neat as possible, wiping off excess glaze that gets on adjacent painted surfaces with a rag.

8. The rich colors of the finish capture the feel of moire, a tone-on-tone fabric. Tone-on-tone offers another benefit: It helps keep irregularities caused by a less-than-steady hand from standing out.

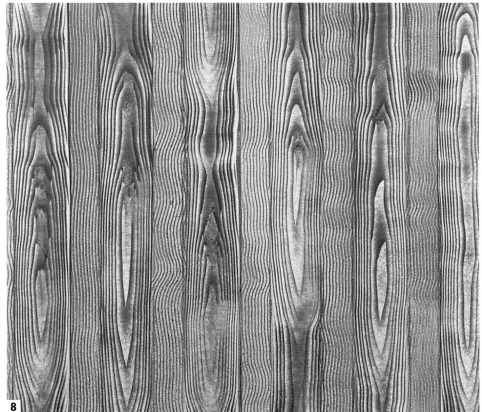

CHAPTER TEN

"TEXTURED" WALL FINISHES

What you do with the walls sets the stage for the look and feel of your rooms. In interior design today, "textures" are hot. You can't pick up a home-design magazine that doesn't show rooms mixing and matching them with ease. "Textured" wall finishes like the ones in this chapter offer simple and affordable ways to introduce the look into your interiors. The finishes are great complements to some of the newest decorating styles. Known as "global" or "ethnic" design, these styles incorporate natural and precious materials and crafts from Africa, Asia, South America, and the Middle East.

If you have just moved into your first home and have little in the way of furnishings, these textured finishes can be a blessing.

The "textured" finish in this blue room gives an airy look to an otherwise small space.

They can dress up and even become the focal point of small, boxy rooms, the eye-catching element guests "ooh and aah" over when they first walk in. The finishes can introduce a sense of quality and originality without sending you over budget.

They can also hold great appeal for the minimalist—whether you're one by choice or have become one out of necessity (as parents of small children often do). If loading a room with lots of (breakable) accessories and (tempting-to-tug-at) window treatments is out of the question, effects like the "Feather-Duster Finish" or "Corduroy Ragging On," are sure ways to inject some life without the fuss.

And they couldn't be more in keeping with today's trend toward relaxed design. Their natural exuberance allows them to hide a multitude of imperfections on walls in poor shape and makes them well suited to spaces that get much use and must serve multiple purposes. And, because you have painted walls, when your tastes change or you move into another life stage, you can alter them more easily than if you have wallpaper or fabric on the walls.

You'll note that the word "textured" appears in quotes here. That's because all the finishes are, of course, flat. The sense of texture comes from the tools and methods with which you apply the glaze to your walls. The finishes in this chapter employ traditional methods of decorative painting, but are often executed with rather untraditional tools, from a paint scraper to plastic wrap. Let this inspire you to try some unconventional tools of your own.

The ragging techniques, traditionally done with cotton cloth or cheesecloth, are particularly open to suggestion. You'll see them using corduroy and plastics here. You can also try paper, lace netting, carpet padding, thin canvas, sisal, or burlap (as long as they don't fray too much).

With all the recipes in this chapter (and in the book), you really need to test your paint colors and tool impressions on paper repeatedly before starting on the walls—especially if you are working with an experimental tool, it may take a while to get the effect you want.

Although these finishes were designed for walls, they can also suit other surfaces, including floors, ceilings, cabinetry, furniture, and accessories. Just be sure to check with your local paint store to get the right paint for your project.

1

RECIPE

FEATHER-DUSTER FINISH

LEVEL OF EXPERTISE:

RECOMMENDED ON: Walls, wall panels

NOT RECOMMENDED ON: Highly carved surfaces, small surfaces

NUMBER OF PEOPLE: 1

TOOLS: Newspapers or drop cloths; paint tray; paint stirrers; roller to apply base coat; paper for testing imprints; mask; rubber gloves; rags for touchup and cleanup; feather duster

 BASE COAT: Coral latex semi-gloss interior house paint

 APPLIED FINISH: Salmon latex semi-gloss interior house paint

GLAZE: Optional

One reason we start this chapter with this finish is to get a point across: Loosen up. You *can* get great effects quickly and easily. You *can* have fun *and* be creative. In decorative painting, anything can serve as a painting tool. Use your imagination, and you may well be pleasantly surprised at what you come up with.

That's exactly what happened here. In Nancy's continuing quest for lively, eye-catching finishes, she took a chance on a feather duster and came up with what can easily be a fast, affordable, and original alternative to wallcovering. Depending on the colors you choose, these feathery impressions can bring to mind anything from a tropical paradise (are those abstract palm trees?) to the retro look of flocked wallpaper. For the feather-duster look, you need to apply only a little paint, hold your tool perpendicular to your surface, and use a light touch. Be sure to practice first on paper.

Also, be sure to make sample boards in the colors you select for your base coat and glaze. As you can see here, this lively finish truly benefits from well-chosen color choices.

1. Pour salmon glaze into paint tray. Hold feather duster perpendicular to paint tray, and dip bottom of feathers into glaze. Make several impressions on paper to test that you have proper amount of paint. Then, working in 3-foot sections, touch feather duster lightly to wall, making imprints several inches apart until you cover entire section.

2. Re-dip feather duster in glaze, and make additional imprints in between those on surface. Continue filling in with imprints until you have overall pattern. Stand back from surface, as needed, to see where you need to fill in.

3. The all-over patterned effect can make a lively substitute for wallpaper.

With any tool that makes a distinct impression (as compared to the muted imprints of a cotton rag), a strong contrast between base-coat and glaze colors can prove overwhelming. Colors from the same family will give you a much softer, effect without relinquishing the "texture."

One last word of advice: Every feather duster is different, so you won't get the exact pattern you see here. Be sure to choose your feather duster with care. As in many decorative painting techniques, you're printing with your tool, and the imprint you get can make or break your finish.

If the duster's feathers are too long, they might droop and give a blurrier effect. This is neither good nor bad—it just means you should test extensively to make sure you're happy with the impression you get. If the impression doesn't suit you, you might try trimming the feathers before you go out and buy another feather duster. Your sample boards are good places to try out your feather-duster tools.

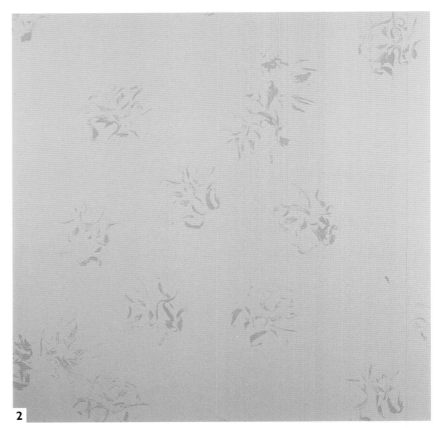

2

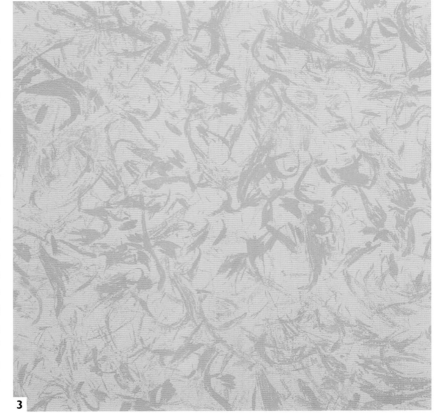

3

RECIPE

CORDUROY RAGGING ON

LEVEL OF EXPERTISE:

RECOMMENDED ON: Walls, panels, cabinetry, furniture, accessories

NOT RECOMMENDED ON: Highly carved surfaces

NUMBER OF PEOPLE: 1 or 2, depending on project size

TOOLS: Newspapers or drop cloths; paint tray; paint stirrers; roller to apply base coat; palette; paper for testing glaze; paint thinner; mask; rubber gloves; rags for touchup and cleanup; corduroy, cut into 12-inch squares; pinking shears and masking tape or lint brush to prepare corduroy

BASE COAT: Plum latex semi-gloss interior house paint

GLAZE: Oil-based glazing liquid and rose oil-based enamel paint

VARNISH: Optional

"Ragging," or cloth distressing, is one of the most popular decorative painting techniques. It is an easy one to master, and once you get comfortable with it, is especially rewarding because you can create so many different looks, depending on the material with which you "rag."

The distinctive finish you see here is a case in point. It's an example of ragging "on"—the additive version of ragging in which you apply glaze over your base coat with a piece of corduroy.

Even within this one technique, you can get different effects, depending on the kind of corduroy you use: Narrow-wale will give you a different pattern from wide-wale. In most cases, the wider the wale, the better. And don't use pin-wale corduroy; it's too thin to give you enough pattern.

For something a little different, try a light glaze over a darker base coat, as you see pictured on the following page. But keep in mind that the closer in color base coat and glaze are, the more subtle the effect. This particularly comes into play if you're using wide-wale corduroy, which gives you a strong pattern. Contrasting colors may make the finish too intense.

Note that when you're working with cloth you need to be extra careful of those foreign particles getting into your finish. Cloth will fray if you don't prepare it carefully. To ready your corduroy, cut it into 12-inch squares, "pinking" the edges with a pinking shears to limit fraying. Next, wash and dry the cloths, then use masking tape or run a lint brush over them to remove as much "fluff" as possible.

How you hold the cloth is key. You want a flat surface to "print" with; so bunch the cloth in your hand, gathering the ends into your palm.

For best results, every time you dip your cloth into the glaze, test it. Use a paper plate or white paper for testing—not newsprint, which could get into the paint.

Be sure to use paint sparingly, and pat cloth lightly against the wall so that the imprint of the fabric remains visible. After dabbing your cloth in the paint, touch it to the wall randomly—this way, the imprints made when the cloth has the most paint on it will be spread over your surface and not concentrated in one spot. Then go back and fill in, continuing until the cloth is almost dry. This is how you get the color variations that add to the finish's distinctive look.

Composition is especially important with this finish. When you apply the glaze, don't limit yourself and work in one tiny area. Keep moving and reaching, up and down, side to side and keep stepping back to see your progress. Distribute the paint well when your cloth is at the same saturation level.

1

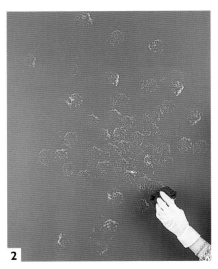

2

3

1. Bunch cloth in your hand to create flat, pillow-like surface, with all ends of rag tucked in. Dip cloth lightly into glaze and test on paper.

2. Press cloth lightly against wall so that imprint from cloth is clearly visible.

3. When you apply glaze, lift the rag and turn wrist so that all your impressions aren't going in same direction. Use glaze sparingly. Touch cloth to wall randomly so that imprints of same color intensity will be spread over surface. Then fill in, continuing until cloth is almost dry. Dip cloth in glaze, test on paper plate, and repeat process on wall. Step back frequently to examine your work.

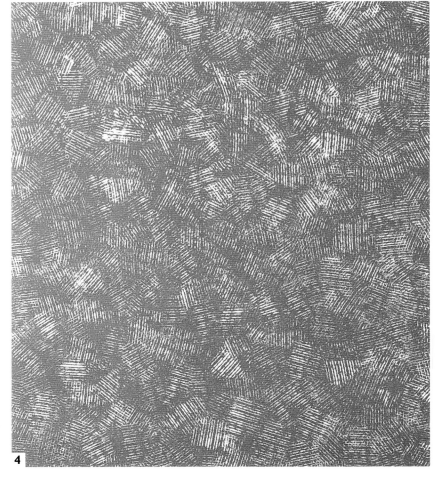

4

4. You can vary this finish by applying a dark color over a light base or by using a different kind of corduroy. (Note, however, that pin-wale corduroy is not recommended; it is probably too thin to supply enough pattern.)

RECIPE

CORDUROY RAGGING OFF

LEVEL OF EXPERTISE:

RECOMMENDED ON:
Walls, wall panels,
cabinetry, furniture,
accessories

NOT RECOMMENDED
ON: Highly carved surfaces

NUMBER OF PEOPLE:
1 or 2, depending on
project size

TOOLS: Newspapers or
drop cloths; paint tray;
paint stirrers; roller to apply
base coat and glaze; paint
thinner; mask; rubber
gloves; rags for touch-up
and cleanup; corduroy,
cut into 12 inch squares;
pinking shears and
lint brush to
prepare corduroy

◆ BASE COAT:
Bone latex semi-
gloss interior
house paint

◆ GLAZE: Oil-based
putty glazing
liquid and alkyd
low-luster
enamel paint

VARNISH: Optional

Before you read any further, turn back to the final shot of the recipe on the previous page, "Corduroy Ragging On." Now look at the finished effect for this recipe. You can't get a much clearer example of what a change in color and a switch from the "additive" to the "subtractive" method of applying glaze will do to a painted finish.

The tool for both finishes is the same: corduroy. But this finish is much more subtle for two reasons: the closer color relationship between the more neutral bone base coat and putty glaze, and the way the glaze is applied. Instead of printing it directly onto the surface with the corduroy, as in the previous recipe, you apply the glaze sub-tractive style: First, apply it over the base coat with a roller, then use your tool (the corduroy) to lift some of it off.

Note that you can get different effects by using other kinds of cor-duroy: narrow-wale, wide-wale, etc. (Pin-wale is probably too thin to provide enough pattern.)

When working with cloth, be extra careful. It can fray and cause bits of fuzz to get into your finish. See the "Corduroy Ragging On" recipe for the best way to make corduroy into a good painting tool.

Watch how you hold the corduroy. To get clear imprints, create a flat surface to remove glaze with; bunch the rest of the cloth in your hand, gathering the ends into your palm.

Ragging off will give you a smoother, more sophisticated look. But keep in mind that, especially on a large surface, it is easiest to do with two people—one to roll on the glaze and the other to remove the glaze before it dries. If you're tackling a project alone, you definitely want to work with oil-based glazes because they take longer to dry and, thus, give you more time for the glaze removal process.

1

1. Remove lint from corduroy with masking tape or lint brush.

2

2. Pour glaze into paint tray. Apply glaze over base coat with roller, criss-crossing strokes to get an even finish.

3. Arrange corduroy in hand to form flat surface. Touch lightly to surface to remove glaze. When cloth is in air, shift hand to get a variety of imprints. Work with same rag until saturated (i. e., when it begins putting glaze back on wall instead of removing it). Then change to new rag, and repeat steps 2 and 3.

3

4. Work in floor-to-ceiling strips of 2 feet to 3 feet. (If you find glaze drying too fast to rag, do smaller sections.) Touch cloth to wall randomly throughout section so that you remove some glaze from all areas when cloth is clean-est. This will keep you from getting a distracting "light spot" in just one area. Stand back regularly to see that smooth overall pattern is developing. But, accept imperfections: Reworking them will remove too much glaze. One rag should last for medium-size wall, but have extras on hand so that you don't run the risk of running out in mid-finish.

5. The finished effect, especially in a room filled with window treatments, furnishings, and accessories, will mask surface imperfections.

4

5

RECIPE

PLASTIC-WRAP RAGGING OFF

LEVEL OF EXPERTISE:

RECOMMENDED ON: Walls

NOT RECOMMENDED ON: Small surfaces

NUMBER OF PEOPLE: 1 or 2, depending on project size

TOOLS: Newspapers or drop cloths; paint tray; paint stirrers; roller to apply base coat; brush to apply glaze; paint thinner; mask; rubber gloves; rags for touchup and cleanup; rolls of plastic wrap (industrial size for large projects)

BASE COAT: Dove white latex semi-gloss interior house paint

GLAZE: Oil-based glazing liquid and rose alkyd low-luster enamel paint

VARNISH: Optional

Through a combination of brush strokes and impressions left by strips of plastic wrap, this finish can give you a pleasing interplay of lights and darks that conveys three-dimensionality.

This finish is a cousin of the leather look you saw in Chapter Nine. However, it has a much stronger "sense of direction," or flow, thanks in part to the way you apply the glaze here—with a brush, all in one direction, instead of with a roller, in several directions.

If you're doing a whole room, you might want to get industrial-size rolls of plastic wrap, available at restaurant supply stores. They make it easier for you to roll out the long strips you'll want for this technique.

You can reuse the same strip of plastic wrap a few times—but not too many because it quickly becomes saturated and stops removing paint.

One important point: If you remove the plastic, and there just isn't enough pattern, you can go back over it with a rag or small piece of plastic wrap while the glaze is still wet. Hold the plastic or rag in the same direction as your finish, and remove more glaze. Work slowly and step back from your surface often so that you can see that you're creating a strong pattern of lights and darks.

1. Over dry base coat, apply glaze with brush. You can apply glaze vertically or horizontally, depending on how you want "stripes" in finish to go. Vary pressure as you paint on glaze to create lighter and darker areas that will add depth to your final finish.

2. Cut off a long strip of plastic wrap and, starting at bottom of wall, stick plastic to glaze. Work your way up wall, smoothing plastic on, but leaving enough "play" in plastic to create crinkles. If you're working by yourself, you'll need to climb up a ladder, keeping hold of plastic, until you reach the ceiling, and then press plastic firmly in place. If you're working in a pair, station one person on ladder and pass plastic strip up.

3. Peel off plastic strip, and stand back to see effect. Adjust your technique on next strip, if needed—i.e., create more crinkles in plastic, press plastic more firmly, etc.

4. Starting from edge of first strip, apply either plastic strip you just removed or use a new strip next to the first, depending on how paint-saturated the plastic is. Repeat process over entire surface.

1

2

3

4

RECIPE

PLASTIC BAG RAGGING OFF

LEVEL OF EXPERTISE:

RECOMMENDED ON: Walls, wall panels, ceilings, cabinetry, furniture, accessories

NOT RECOMMENDED ON: Highly carved surfaces

NUMBER OF PEOPLE: 1

TOOLS: Newspapers or drop cloths; paint tray; paint stirrers; roller to apply base coat; brush to apply glaze; paint thinner; mask; rubber gloves; rags for touchup and cleanup; plastic bags

BASE COAT: Robin's egg blue latex semi-gloss interior house paint

 GLAZE: Oil-based moss green glazing liquid and oil-based paint

VARNISH: Optional

Here's the traditional "subtractive" technique of ragging off executed with an untraditional material—plastic sandwich bags. The bags give you a finish with extra depth and a more pronounced texture than you would get if you used the soft cotton rags usually associated with this technique.

Working with plastic has its advantages. For one, the bags are easier to crumple up in your hand than cloth. And you don't have to prepare them like you do cloth—they come out of the box lint-free and cut to size. Because plastic doesn't absorb glaze like cloth does, however, you'll need more of them than you would cloth. And keep in mind the effect changing bags will have on your finish: A fresh bag will lift off more glaze, so don't make all of your marks with a new bag in one spot.

Remember that because this is a subtractive technique—glaze is applied over the base coat with a paint roller, then removed with the plastic bags—it is best executed by two. However, for a small project, you can go it alone.

A major contributor to the depth and richness of the finish pictured here is the color choice. The warm green glaze, with a hint of the blue base coat peeking through, is a great example of what decorative painting has to offer over flat-painted surfaces.

The glowing color that results when the eye combines the transparent layers of this finish would be a wonderful complement to the deep red, blue, and green hues of a "jewel-tone" color scheme or an English hunting-lodge style interior, either for the main elements like the walls or on eye-catching accents.

1. Pour glaze into paint tray. Apply over base coat with roller, criss-crossing your strokes to get an even finish.

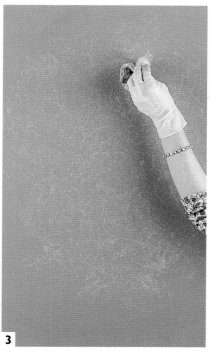

2

3

4

2. Crumple plastic bag in your hand so that you have a lot of wrinkles in part of bag that will touch surface. Press bag lightly to surface to remove glaze. When bag is off surface, turn your wrist, and sometimes your arm, to vary impressions made in glaze.

3. Work in floor-to-ceiling strips about 2-feet to 3-feet wide. (If glaze dries too fast, do smaller sections.) Use same bag until saturated; when it stops removing glaze from surface, use another bag. Touch bag to wall randomly throughout section so that you remove some glaze from all areas when bag is cleanest and thus removes most.

4. Stand back to check if pattern is developing evenly. Don't rework sections; you will remove too much glaze. In the finished effect, small imperfections blend in.

RECIPE

SPATTERING IN FOUR COLORS

LEVEL OF EXPERTISE:

RECOMMENDED ON: Walls

NUMBER OF PEOPLE: 1

TOOLS: Newspapers or drop cloths; paint tray; paint stirrers; roller to apply base coat; mask; rubber gloves; rags for touchup and cleanup; heavy-duty stripping tool and pads

BASE COAT: Butter latex semi-gloss interior house paint

APPLIED FINISH: Latex semi-gloss interior house paint in 4 colors

◆ Sunflower

◆ Dusty rose

◆ Robin's egg blue

◆ Teal

VARNISH: Optional

eed a quick-and-clever way to liven up a child's room? Try this recipe for spattering in a bunch of bright hues. Set against a lively yellow ground, the four colors used here—sunflower, dusty rose, robin's egg blue, and teal—convey youthful exuberance without screaming "children's room." The finish can be a more sophisticated alternative to juvenile wallcovering in a room filled with furnishings in primary colors—one that a child won't outgrow as fast and that can more easily accommodate changes in decor.

This recipe also offers another example of how something you might have around the house can help give you an original finish with ease. Nancy isn't quite certain what made her decide to experiment with a heavy-duty paint-stripping pad, but we're sure glad she did. Her unusual choice of a painting tool, readily available in paint, hardware, and home stores, let her create the appealing finish you see here.

Her technique is actually a cross between two classic decorative-painting techniques—spattering and stippling—but much faster and easier than either of them, especially on large surfaces. And compared to traditional methods of spattering, this one is neater—glaze doesn't fly all over when you dab it on like this, compared to when you bang or flick it off the bristles of a brush.

Note that you can get a similar effect from the kind of brush you use to clean an outdoor grill. But before you go and buy one, maybe you should check what else you have around the house. you never know what kind of finish you might come up with!

Bright hues aren't the only colors this finish looks great in. Take a look at our second "serving suggestion," "Blue Spatter Finish" as shown in a range of blues on page 150. It's a perfect foil to the perennially popular blue-and-white decorating scheme. But don't stop there. This simple-to-achieve effect offers myriad possibilities.

One last tip: When executing this finish, have patience. It does not acquire all its "oomph" until the end. It builds up gradually, layer upon layer, and the final result is enhanced by the way your eye visually "mixes" all those dots of color.

1. Pour first glaze color into paint tray. Dip stripping tool straight down into glaze. Dab off excess glaze on top of paint tray and on paper until imprints have "spattered" look.

2. Touch tool to wall, straight on, repeatedly. Working in 3-foot sections, make imprints over section randomly so that imprints made when tool has most paint on it are spread throughout.

3. Repeat process with second, third, and fourth glaze colors, cleaning or changing pad on stripping tool between each one. Because the amount you're applying is minute, glazes dry quickly, so you don't have to wait before beginning the next spattering layer.

4. Step back as you work to insure you are creating an even pattern over your surface.

SERVING SUGGESTION

BLUE SPATTER FINISH

If collecting blue-and-white ware is your passion, or if you like that "summer house" feeling all year 'round, you'll love this soft and subtle version of the spattered finish. Done in four shades of blue, from dark to light, it can be the perfect foil for furnishings, window treatments, and accessories with a blue-and-white theme. For tools, step-by-step instructions, etc., see "Spattering In Four Colors," page 148.

BASE COAT: White linen latex semi-gloss interior house paint

APPLIED FINISH: 4 latex flat paint colors

 Sail blue

 Cornflower

 Navy

 Delft blue

RECIPE

FLOGGING

LEVEL OF EXPERTISE:

RECOMMENDED ON: Walls

NUMBER OF PEOPLE: 2 recommended, but can be done with 1

TOOLS: Newspapers or drop cloths; rags; rollers to apply base coat and glaze; paint trays; paint stirrers; paint thinner; mask; rubber gloves; containers for mixing glazes in; flogging brush or 2-inch house-painting brush with extra-long bristles; 1-inch foam brush

◆ BASE COAT: White linen latex semi-gloss interior house paint

GLAZES: Oil-based glazing liquid and 2 alkyd low-luster paint colors

◆ Mustard

◆ Brown

VARNISH: Optional

This technique is a good example of how one decorative finish can lead to another. "Flogging" is an intriguing effect in its own right; but it is also the background for "Leopard skin," which you'll find in the *Stenciling* chapter. "Flogging" creates a "furry" background over which to apply the leopard's stenciled spots.

Having the right tool for the job is often the key to success. But here, the right tool could easily break the budget. It is called a "flogging" brush, and what makes it great are its 5-inch-long bristles. In this technique, you manipulate the glaze by striking the surface with your brush; the bristles on a flogging brush are long enough so that you don't get the mark of the metal band that holds the bristles in place. As a substitute, choose a much-less-expensive 2-inch house-painting brush with the longest bristles you can find.

This recipe would be much more difficult to execute with water-based glazes. Oil-based glazes stay wet much longer and give you enough time to manipulate them.

The depth of this finish comes from the range in opacity of your glazes. You'll use several, from brown glaze comprising mostly glazing liquid to brown paint right from the can. In all cases, only apply a little glaze at a time.

If you are creating this finish to "stand alone," you, of course, have total freedom in its look. But if it will be the background for leopard skin, study the photo of leopard skin shown on page 172 first. You want to capture the "furry" feeling.

The surface needs to be spotty, but there doesn't need to be any pattern to it. Patches should vary in size. Stand back to check if your light and dark areas fall in pleasing ways. There are actually two distinct flogging stages to this recipe. If you aren't using this as a background for leopard skin, you may prefer to stop after step 3. This gives you a more pronounced, "random-brushed" effect with stronger contrasts among glaze colors. Following the rest of the steps on these pages will give a smoother, softer, more fully blended finish.

1. With a roller, apply mustard glaze to surface. Then, while glaze is still wet, start at top of surface and "drag" 2-inch house-painting brush down over glaze. Then, "flog" glaze in rows. ("Flog" means to hit or beat the surface quickly with the side of the bristle of the brush.) Let dry thoroughly.

2. Mix about four brown glazes, using the same color paint but varying the amount of glazing liquid from mostly glazing liquid to brown paint straight from can. Using just a little glaze at a time, apply paint in patches by dabbing tip and sides of 1-inch foam brush on surface.

3. Immediately "flog" paint patches with 2-inch house-painting brush. Vary size of patches. Be sure to leave some mustard glaze visible.

4. Working with foam brush in one hand and house-painting brush in other hand, apply more of each brown glaze in same manner, but taking off less paint. Instead of patting surface, just brush it lightly. Let dry thoroughly. To continue with "Leopard skin" recipe, turn to page 173.

CHAPTER ELEVEN

SMALL-SURFACE SPECIALTIES & STENCILING

What do you do if you love antique furniture, but can't afford to buy period pieces? What do you do if you've always wanted fine moldings or charming handpainted designs gracing your home? You don't have to be an artist to achieve the beautiful results found on the following pages.

Three traditional techniques can add classic looks and fine details to worn or dated surroundings. Two are small-surface specialties— decoupage and crackle glazing— that can transform ordinary objects into new family heirlooms. The third, stenciling offers an easy and affordable substitute for wallpaper or fine moldings, and can give plain furniture an appealing folk art look.

But these recipes can do more than antique: They can also be used to create the most modern styles, just by using updated patterns and colors.

While working with these techniques is easy, painting the overall paint coats on some objects and furniture may prove challenging for the novice decorative painter. Take preparation work seriously—in decorative painting, it's a major ingredient of your end result. Although the crackle glaze can hide, and in some cases even be enhanced by, surface imperfections, too many might cause the finish to peel. And with decoupage, your pasted-on designs might not adhere properly. See Chapter Three, *Preparing To Paint*, for additional help in this area. Also make sure you have paint that is compatible with your piece.

Oil-based paint is considered more durable and, therefore, recommended for pieces such as chairs, that will be often used. Varnish also serves as a finish protector on pieces you'll handle daily. See *Mixing Paints* for further guidance.

Through decorative painting, a simple shape like this pedestal can be transformed into something just as special as the object that it displays.

RECIPE

CRACKLE GLAZE

LEVEL OF EXPERTISE:

RECOMMENDED ON: Furniture, accessories, molding, cabinetry

NOT RECOMMENDED ON: Floors

NUMBER OF PEOPLE: 1

TOOLS: Newspaper or drop cloths; small power sander; sand paper; tack cloth; paint tray; paint stirrers; paint thinner to clean up oil base coat; water to clean up latex paint and crackle glaze; mask; rubber gloves; 1 1/2-inch nylon sash brush for glazing; 1 1/2-inch Chinese bristle brush for base coat

BASE COAT: Palamino brown oil-based eggshell paint

APPLIED FINISH: Layer of latex-based crackle glaze (see *Sources*, page 185), then layer of hazelnut latex paint

VARNISH: Use water-based varnish

That much-sought-after "patina of age" made easy —that's what this finish is all about. Here, a flea-market find takes on the persona of a prized antique with an off-the-shelf glazing product and a few simple steps.

Remember, however, that the piece you choose to work on must be in good condition to merit such a transformation because although the process is not difficult, it is time consuming—especially all the sanding it sometimes takes to get a piece ready. Before you transform anything, be sure it is structurally sound.

Also consider that if this is your first attempt at painting furniture, you may want to do a practice run on something smaller. Consider buying a small unpainted wooden box, like those you can buy at craft shops, to test your skills on first.

There are recipes for making your own crackle glaze but, as this project shows, off-the-shelf products work perfectly well. If, however, you can't find ready-made crackle glaze in paint or hobby shops in your area, you may be able to get one through mail order (see *Sources*).

To get results like you see here, you can just use the glaze straight from the can. For finer cracks, you can thin the molasses-like glaze from its gummy state to the consistency of syrup (but no thinner) with water. Thinning the glaze will cause it to drip even more than it's already inclined to do; but don't worry— the drips won't show much because of the crackled surface.

What causes the cracks is no deep, dark secret, but rather a common effect one usually tries to avoid. You can get a similarly cracked surface—although not as

consistently—just by applying a latex-based paint over an oil-based paint.

Colorwise, you'll probably get the best success by using a lighter and darker shade of the same color. Either the lighter or darker shade can be the base coat; experiment to see which you prefer.

One last tip—if you do use two colors close in tone, and you want to give your work a true "antiqued" look, go with optional step 3: Before you varnish, use a cotton rag to rub on a thin layer of your base coat in places to create a distressed look.

To begin, paint your base coat. (Remember to paint underside of the chair.) Let dry completely overnight, if possible. Then sand piece (with power sander or by hand, depending on size of piece), and wipe with a tack cloth to insure next coat will adhere.

1

2

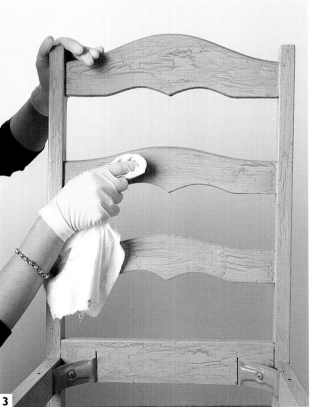

3

1. Paint on crackle glaze in smooth layer. Let dry thoroughly (overnight).

2. Apply coat of latex paint. Crackling will begin almost immediately. Smooth paint on with easy, sweeping strokes, painting in direction of wood grain as much as possible. Avoid going back over your work. Let dry thoroughly (overnight is recommended).

3. If desired, use a cotton rag to rub on random patches of your base coat color for a more "aged" look.

4. With paint pad, apply coat of water-based varnish to insure durability of finish. Finished effect gives an antiqued feel.

RECIPE

DECOUPAGE

LEVEL OF EXPERTISE:

RECOMMENDED ON:
Furniture, cabinetry, accessories including trays, boxes, screens, lamps

NOT RECOMMENDED ON: Floors, highly carved surfaces

NUMBER OF PEOPLE: 1

TOOLS: Newspaper or drop cloths; small power sander; sandpaper; tack cloth; paint tray; paint stirrers; paint thinner; mask; rubber gloves; 12-inch-square cotton rags; small artist's bristle brush for putting in lines; pictures to paste down; scissors or craft knife to cut out pictures; pencil or chalk marker; white glue; toothpicks and/or fine paint brush to apply glue to back of pictures

BASE COAT: Almond spray paint

GLAZE: Oil-based glazing liquid & white oil-base enamel paint

 LINING: Dark green oil-base enamel paint

VARNISH: Use water-based varnish

Handpainted furniture is so popular today, but what if you can't paint? In this recipe, you'll learn one way to get the look.

This recipe borrows a technique from history: decoupage. In 18th-century Europe, decoupage regularly stood in for hand-painting on fashionable lacquered furniture, and it became a favored pastime among craft-loving Victorian women.

Although easier by far than painting on decoration, decoupage isn't just fun and games. With this technique, neatness counts. How carefully you cut out your shapes, how meticulously you prepare your surface, and how well you apply the several coats of varnish required will determine your end result.

These wood nesting tables, a fleamarket find, required good surface preparation. The tables were sanded, first with a small power sander and then by hand, and wiped with a sticky tack cloth to remove particles, the scourge of decorative painting. The investment of time and energy was well worth it because the smoother your surface, the better the finish looks and the more durable the finish is because subsequent paint layers find it easier to adhere. (For a more detailed guide to surface preparation, see Chapter Three.)

The almond-colored base coat demonstrates another way to apply paint: It was sprayed on. Over that is a decorative finish called "ragging on." One of the simplest techniques, it is the same method used in "Corduroy Ragging On," and plays a role in several other recipes in this book.

A good idea when picking background colors for your decoupage project is to take a cue from the background color of the motifs you cut out and do a mottled-color (i.e., ragged, sponged, marbled, etc.) version of that. Note, however, that traditionally decoupage was done on a plain painted background, and you can easily do the same.

For this particular decoupage project, the arrangement of the flower shapes plays a big role in its appeal. But, if you're concerned your "artistic eye" isn't yet up to it, you might prefer to use simpler shapes and place them randomly.

In your search for just the right motifs, check out old books, gift wrap, greeting cards, old-fashioned valentines, playing cards, cotton fabrics, and black-and-white or color photographs. Using matchbook covers, postcards, or even business cards could turn a table into a memory keeper. If you want to use pictures from magazines or newspapers, however, be sure to test first; applying glue and varnish to the thin paper may make the image on the back of the picture show through.

Varnishing is at the heart of this technique. You'll apply numerous coats to protect your handiwork. There are a number of varnishes you can use, but water-based has its advantages. For one thing, it's easy to clean up. And it's low-luster; many oil-based varnishes give surfaces a high shine that you may not want for your project.

1. **Prepare surface by sanding and then remove particles with tack cloth. Spray paint almond base coat and let dry. In paint tray, mix 20 percent white oil-based enamel paint and 80 percent glazing liquid; thin to consistency of milk. Crumple 12-inch-square cotton rag loosely in your hand. Dip rag in glaze, and dab off on paper, testing impression. Touch rag lightly to table or object, "ragging on" over entire surface. Let dry overnight.**

2. **With light-tack masking tape, cover areas you don't want to get paint on, then paint in lines with dark green oil-based paint and small flat bristle brush, using small, short strokes. Paint over edge of tape to be sure you don't miss any spots. Press tape into place firmly to prevent seepage. But be prepared for seepage by having your base color on hand for touchups. (Note: On this piece, lines are recessed and thus easier to paint; so extensive masking wasn't required.) Let dry thoroughly.**

3

4

5

6

3. With craft knife or scissors, cut out pictures you will use for decoupage. Before applying glue, lay out pieces to see where you want them to go and mark their positions very lightly on your surface.

4. Mix a little water into glue so that it spreads more easily. Apply glue to back of pictures with paint brush or toothpick, depending on size of piece. Press pictures in place. Let dry. Make sure they are laying flat.

5. Apply three to ten coats of varnish to pieces, sanding lightly and wiping with tack cloth between coats for better adherence. Let dry thoroughly between coats.

6. The decoupage technique lets you get a hand-painted look even if you're not an artist.

A Guide to Stenciling

WHICH STENCILING PROJECT TO DO

Stenciling is easy, but it can also be time consuming. What takes the most time are multi-color stencils—such as the architectural molding—because for each color you must cut and work with an additional stencil. Before you start, decide how much time you can invest, keeping in mind that you can get great results in good time with a single-color motif—like the tile design included here.

With multi-color stencils, you must also pay strict attention to registration—the way each stencil aligns on top of the previous one. This is crucial to a professional look. To make this happen, in each stencil, you will cut out registration marks that help keep the alignment precise. Be sure to paint in those marks before starting on the rest of the stencil.

USING THE STENCILS IN THIS BOOK

You'll find patterns for each of the stencils starting on page 178. Just enlarge or reduce them to the size you need for your project on a photocopy machine.

Next, transfer the patterns to either acetate or stenciling cardboard, both available at craft shops and some art stores. Which material to use depends on the project you select. In each recipe, a material is specified. Substitutions are perfectly permissible—although with multi-color stencils, see-through acetate makes alignment easier. See the next page for step-by-step instructions on transferring and cutting out stencils on both acetate and cardboard.

Cutting stencils can be tricky, especially if there are lots of curved lines and little "bridges," those small areas that hold the elements of your pattern together.

Practice first. Nancy found that a new electric stencil-cutting tool, available by mail, by Air Nouveau, made the job much easier; she demonstrates it on the next page. (See *Sources*, page 185, for ordering information.)

Two tips: Use masking tape to mend your stencil if you make a mistake. And for rounded edges, you might find it a bit easier to turn the stencil instead of moving your knife.

Especially for multi-color stencil projects, after cutting out the stencils, you should always number them and mark them with the words "front," "top," and "right." This aids in aligning them properly. (Especially in the heat of the project, mix-ups have been known to occur.)

CHOOSING PAINTS AND TOOLS

Although you can stencil with other tools—paint brushes, sponges, and spray paint—stenciling brushes are good investments. The popularity of stenciling has made these round brushes with flat surfaces more readily available; check craft and art supply shops, as well as mail-order catalogs (see *Sources*, page 185).

As with regular brushes, you can get stenciling brushes in nylon for use with water-based paints and bristle for oil-based paints. They come in a wide range of sizes. The size to choose depends on your project; a larger brush can make a project go faster.

You can buy special stenciling paints, but you can also get good results with latex paint, water-based artist's acrylics, or oil-based "japan colors," available in art supply stores.

A cardinal rule with stenciling: Use only a little paint at a time so that it doesn't seep under the stencil and ruin your design. And note that you can vary the pressure with which you apply the paint to change the look: For instance, you can create a "fade-away" effect by dabbing your brush more firmly at the center of your design and lightening your touch as you move toward the edges. Experimenting with brushes and paints will make your stencil look unique.

KEEPING STENCILS IN PLACE

A quick tip to make stenciling easier: Use light-tack stenciling adhesive spray to keep your stencil in place. If you have a large stencil and find it pulling away from your surface, back up the adhesive with masking tape. Note that when spraying adhesive, you should always wear a protective mask.

RECIPE

TRANSFERRING AND CUTTING A STENCIL FROM CARDBOARD

Using a photocopy machine, make several copies of the pattern you would like to use. You'll only need one copy of each part of the pattern, but it's a good idea to have extra copies on hand in case you make a tough-to-repair mistake in cutting. You can either keep the stencil pattern the same size, reduce it, or enlarge it, depending on the scale of your project.

TOOLS: Several photocopies of stencil pattern; cardboard; scissors; light-tack stenciling adhesive spray; craft knife

Spray adhesive on the back of a photocopy. Press the copy down onto cardboard cut to the width of your stencil. It's easier to leave the cardboard extra long until you've cut out your stencil so that you have something to hold on to. Cut out white areas of the stencil using a craft knife. Be sure to cut out registration marks, if indicated.

RECIPE

TRANSFERRING AND CUTTING A STENCIL FROM ACETATE

TOOLS: Photocopies of stencil pattern; acetate, available in rolls or sheets; posterboard, about size of stencil pattern; scissors; light-tack stenciling adhesive spray; piece of window glass; masking tape; electric stencil-cutting tool or craft knife

Spray adhesive on back of a photocopy trimmed roughly to size of stencil pattern. Place copy on top of posterboard, pressing it into place. Place photocopy under piece of glass. With scissors, cut acetate a little larger than size of stencil. With masking tape, tape acetate down on top of glass, centered over photocopy. Plug in cutting tool. When hot, use it to cut out stencil pattern, moving slowly along outside edge of white elements of design. (See page 164 for tips on cutting along curves.)

RECIPE

TILE

LEVEL OF EXPERTISE:

RECOMMENDED ON: Walls, wall panels, floors, borders, fireplace surrounds, countertops, tabletops, furnishings

NOT RECOMMENDED ON: Highly carved surfaces

NUMBER OF PEOPLE: I

TOOLS: Newspapers or drop cloths; rags; roller for applying base coat; paint tray; paint stirrers; rubber gloves; stenciling cardboard; craft knife; cutting board; light-tack stenciling adhesive spray; masking tape; I-inch nylon stenciling brush; palette; paper for testing brushes on; level; large foam brush for varnishing

BASE COAT: Celery latex semi-gloss interior house paint

APPLIED FINISH: Tan latex semi-gloss interior house paint

VARNISH: Use water-based varnish

Always wanted a tile back-splash behind your stove? Why not stencil one in? This original stenciled design easily captures the look and feel of tile. You can use it to cover a wall, border a room, or arranged in a simple group of four, as pictured here, serve as an elegant inset panel.

You'll find the pattern for this stencil on page 178. Just remove it from the book and enlarge or reduce it on a photocopy machine depending on your needs. Then transfer the pattern onto stenciling cardboard and cut it out, following the instructions on page 165. Mark on stencil the words "front," "top," and "right" so that it can be aligned easily each time. (See page 164 for additional guidelines.)

A big plus with this design: You only use one stencil so you don't have to align another stencil precisely on top of it. And since this interlocking pattern is a simple repeat, you just move the stencil over and put it down the same way each time.

To line up your stenciling for smaller projects, you'll need just a level and masking tape. Apply horizontal and vertical lines of tape to the surface where you want your stenciling to be, then adjust the tape using the level until the lines are straight.

With that method, you avoid marking your surface. For an entire room, however, you'll need to draw in pencil or chalk guidelines. Put them in as lightly as possible (you may need to paint over the pencil after stenciling).

1. Spray adhesive on back of stencil. Put up masking tape guidelines, checking them with level.

2. Flatten stencil carefully against wall, lining it up against bottom edge of tape line you applied to your surface. Put paint on palette. Dab stenciling brush lightly in paint, then dab on paper until brush is almost dry. Dab brush over stencil, covering surface thoroughly. Lift off stencil and, keeping stencil in same position, place down next to first print; repeat process until your surface is completed.

3. Arranged in a simple group of four, the stencil becomes an elegant insert panel.

RECIPE

GRAPE-LEAF MOTIF

LEVEL OF EXPERTISE:

RECOMMENDED ON:
Walls, wall panels, floors, ceilings, door and window surrounds, fireplace surrounds, furnishings, accessories

NOT RECOMMENDED ON:
Highly carved surfaces

NUMBER OF PEOPLE: 1

TOOLS: Newspapers or drop cloths; rags for touchup; paint stirrers; paint tray; light-tack masking tape to hold stencil in place; rubber gloves; one 12-inch by 18-inch piece of acetate for main stencil, plus 5 smaller pieces for detail stencils; craft knife; cutting board; 2 bristle stenciling brushes, 1-inch or larger; 2 palettes; paper for testing on

◇ BASE COAT:
Dove white latex flat interior house paint

GLAZES: For ragged background—50 percent flat latex interior house paint and 50 percent water—2 colors

◇ Pearl

◇ Sky blue

STENCIL PAINTS: Plaid brand acrylic stencil paints

(5 "grape" colors)—

 Royal violet

 Heather

 Lavender

 Blue ink

 Tapestry wine

4 shades of green—

◇ Basil

 Indian

 Hunter

 Thicket

VARNISH: Optional

Love the hand-painted look, but don't consider yourself an artist? No problem. Use this stencil as a jumping-off point.

The stencil—consisting of a main pattern and several smaller elements (leaves, grapevine)—gives you the basic forms and helps you keep those forms consistent throughout your project—often a challenge for beginning painters. (For instance, if you're framing a doorway, it can insure that the first leaves you paint, on one side of the doorway, will look like the last leaves you paint, on the other side.)

Then, by stenciling over the shapes in several colors instead of one, you can easily give your design a sense of depth. There's no reason stenciling has to be "flat;" the building-up adds interest and makes a design unique.

Finally, by painting in simple details, such as wavy lines for veining on leaves, you can capture the hand-done look. To see how far you can go with this, turn to the photo of the designer-showhouse room on page 116. Nancy and Jeffrey Brooks, the interior designer of the room, assisted Nick Devlin, the mural painter, by stenciling in individual leaf shapes for the background of the grapevine. Nick went over every leaf, hand-painting in detail on the stenciling and filling in the grapevine structure and background. (For another look at how to hand-paint veining, see the *"Fantasy" Marbling* chapter.)

This stencil is a charmer. It features one of today's most fashionable motifs: fruit designs.

Another part of the stencil's charm comes from its free-flowing nature. It is especially fun to do because it is much less rigid. You don't need to register it or arrange it in a straight row, and you can put the next motif wherever you want. For instance, you can apply all or parts of the main motif to walls randomly (instead of evenly spaced or in rows) to create your own original wallcovering.

The pattern for this stencil is on page 179. Enlarge or reduce them on a photocopy machine, if needed, to fit your space. Then transfer the patterns to acetate and cut them out.

Because you'll want to flip the stencil over and use it on the other side to get different angles, don't spray the back with stenciling adhesive to hold it in place. Use light-tack masking tape.

The instructions for this recipe include how to paint the "sky" background. You can, of course, put this stencil over any background, whether solid or "broken" color or plain wood.

To get a cloudy look, make the the blue and white paint for the sky very transparent by watering it down to a 50/50 mix with water. And apply paint by dabbing it lightly on your surface with a sea sponge, preferably one with a lot of holes in it.

(Note: This technique is called "sponging on." For more tips on sponging on, see the "Stucco" recipe and the *Fantasy* *Marbling* chapter. For a detailed review of sponging, see Chapter Five in the first volume of *Recipes for Surfaces*.)

1. In paint tray, mix 50 percent sky blue latex paint and 50 percent water. Wet sea sponge, and wring out. Dip sponge in paint, then off-load most of paint onto paper. Touch sponge to wall lightly, turning your wrist when sponge is in air to vary impressions. Cover much of pearl base coat with blue. Let paint dry. (This will happen quickly, before you're ready to start your next coat.)

2. In paint tray, mix half pearl latex paint and half water. Rinse out sponge, and wring well. Dip in paint, off-load excess on paper. Touch lightly to wall in areas where sky blue is heaviest to bring back some of base-coat color.

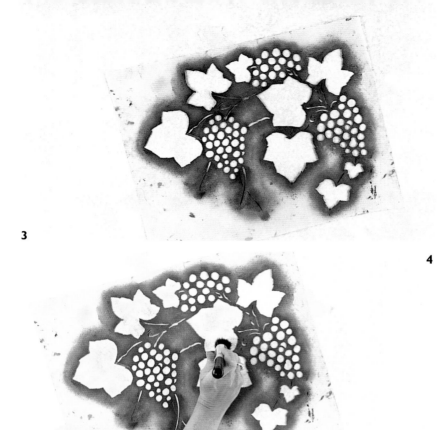

3

3. With masking tape, position main stencil on wall in your starting position. Prepare palette with four shades of green paint.

4

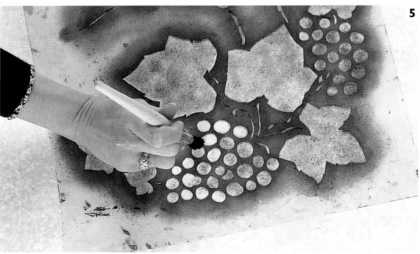

4. Dab stencil brush into one green color and blot off excess on paper until brush is almost dry. Dab brush over leaves. Repeat with next three green colors, one on top of the other. (Because you use so little paint, previous color should be dry by the time you're on to next.)

5. Set up palette with five "grape" paint colors. Dab second stenciling brush into one color, blot off excess on paper, then dab over grapes. Repeat process with other five grape colors. Note: Don't go over every grape in all five colors. Variations enhance the look. Make some more red or purple; even green.

5

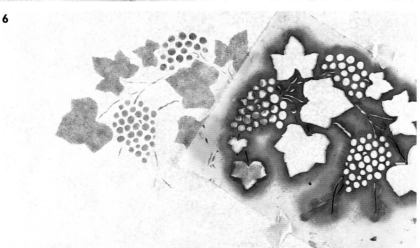

6. Remove stencil and move to next spot, taping in place. If you're placing stencil next to first design, you can overlap it slightly; but make sure none of the previous design shows through in the areas you will stencil next. Note: It's not necessary to do whole next stencil; you may prefer just to do some leaves, or skip one bunch of grapes. Step back and view pattern you're creating.

6

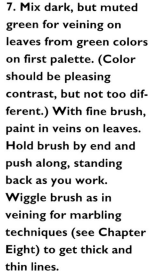

7. Mix dark, but muted green for veining on leaves from green colors on first palette. (Color should be pleasing contrast, but not too different.) With fine brush, paint in veins on leaves. Hold brush by end and push along, standing back as you work. Wiggle brush as in veining for marbling techniques (see Chapter Eight) to get thick and thin lines.

8. Using separate detail stencil, put in some grape vines using medium-green paint.

9. Add in separate stencils of leaves where desired—in a corner, for example, where main stencil might not fit. Or, on the floor nearby, as if single leaf had fallen off vine. Then paint in veining.

10. Final shot shows just one of the many looks you can get with this stencil, from the very flat to lifelike. Consider painting in white lattice-work over sky, then applying grape stencils. Get leaf structure in place first, then add in details—full vines, branches, artist style shading to make grapes appear round (look at still life paintings for inspiration).

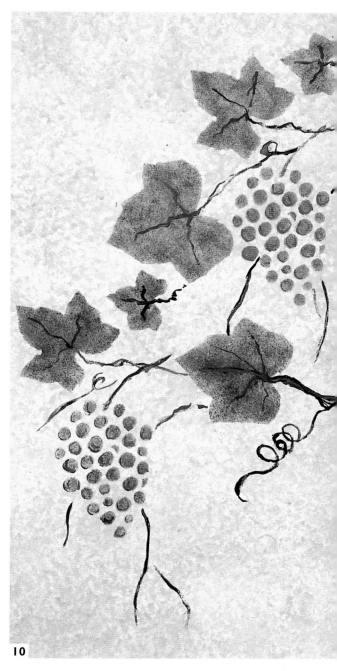

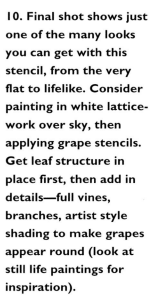

RECIPE

LEOPARD SKIN

LEVEL OF EXPERTISE:

RECOMMENDED ON: Walls, wall panels, furnishings, accessories

NOT RECOMMENDED ON: Highly carved surfaces

NUMBER OF PEOPLE: 1

TOOLS: Newspapers or drop cloths; rags for touchup; paint stirrers; paint thinner; mask; rubber gloves; 12-inch by 18-inch sheet of acetate; craft knife; cutting board; removable artist's adhesive spray; masking tape; 1-inch bristle stenciling brushes; palette; paper for testing brushes on; level

BASE COAT: White linen latex semi-gloss interior house paint; alkyd low-luster interior house paint; and oil-based enamel paint— see "Flogging" recipe, page 151.

 STENCILING: Chocolate oil-based paint

GLAZE: Oil-based glazing liquid and 2 alkyd low-luster paints

 Mustard

 Brown

VARNISH: Optional

Exotic animal prints are finding a home in many decorating styles. A wall of stenciled leopard skin might make an ideal backdrop for modern furnishings or the latest revivals. Animal prints are also a natural with "global" settings, those inspired by cultural and ethnic influences from distant corners of the world, as well as "environmental" interiors, which emphasize natural materials and earth tones. And leopard skin accents—from a stenciled tabletop to an old hatbox—sit well with styles as diverse as British Colonial, retro-1950s, and Country.

On page 180, you'll find the pattern for this stencil. Follow the instructions for cutting out a stencil on acetate, a clear material available in sheets or rolls at art or craft stores. (See page 165 for more on cutting out stencils.)

Be sure to cut out the registration marks on the four sides of this stencil; these small notches are vital to lining up your stencil precisely each time. When you move your stencil, don't overlap it.

You can see what a beautiful effect you can get with this stencil from the pictures. But what you can't tell is how easy it is. Usually, to look this good, faux leopard skin needs to have overlapping spots—which would require cutting and using two stencils. Here, you need only one.

The key to this is the background. It's what gives the finish its almost furry look, as well as its range of lights and darks. You'll find the recipe for the background, called "Flogging," in the chapter on *"Textured" Wall Finishes.* That's because the background works so well as a finish in its own right. To get the leopard skin look you see here, start there.

Note that if you can't find acetate, you can cut this stencil out of cardboard. Acetate, however, is easier to work with because you can see through it. Another option is to substitute spray paint for oil-based paint; on a large surface, this would be a time saver.

1

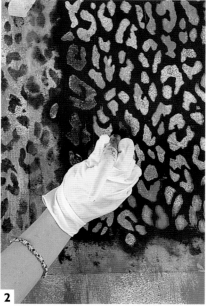

2

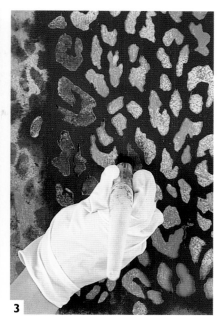

3

1. Wearing mask and gloves, spray back of stencil with adhesive. Mark guidelines lightly on surface so that the first time you put your stencil down it is plumb and level. After that, each time you move stencil, align it with last. (Note: Elaborate measuring isn't necessary; pattern hides variations.) Use masking tape, if necessary, to insure stencil stays in place. Put paint on palette. Dip 1-inch stenciling brush in paint, then "off-load" extra paint onto test paper or paper plate.

2. Dab brush lightly over surface, filling in stencil pattern. Then move stencil to adjacent spot; put masking tape under registration marks and paint over marks.

3. Repeat stencil process until background is covered. Let dry thoroughly. Paint over registration marks first.

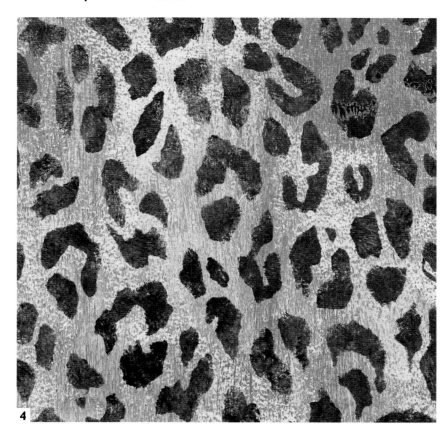

4

4. To get this rich pattern with great depth required only one stencil, applied over an easy-to-execute "flogged" background.

RECIPE

ARCHITECTURAL MOLDING

LEVEL OF EXPERTISE:

RECOMMENDED ON: Room border at ceiling height

NOT RECOMMENDED ON: Floors, small or highly carved surfaces

NUMBER OF PEOPLE: 1

TOOLS: Newspapers or drop cloths; rags for touchup and cleanup; paint tray; paint roller for applying base coat; paint stirrers; rubber gloves; package of cheesecloth, cut into 24-inch squares; large sheet of acetate to cut three stencils from; craft knife; cutting board; light-tack stenciling adhesive spray; masking tape; 3 1-inch nylon stenciling brushes, 1 for each glaze color; palette; paper for testing

BASE COAT: Coffee latex flat interior house paint

APPLIED FINISH: Latex flat interior house paint in 4 colors

 Pearl (for cheeseclothing)

 Latte

Cappucino

Espresso

VARNISH: Optional

You can find stencils everywhere, but it's not often you see an architectural stencil like this egg-and-dart crown molding Nancy designed. This stencil can easily stand alone at the ceiling line of a room. Or, if you're lucky enough to have molding already in place, as shown here, you can use the stencil to add extra character.

Stenciled or otherwise, crown molding can transform a room. It can help turn a plain setting into a proper showcase for classic furnishings. It can make a small, boxy interior seem more spacious by drawing the eye upward.

The colors chosen for this stencil contribute greatly to the finished effect. They help convey a sense of depth by creating highlights and shadows like those you'd find on old molding carved long ago from stone.

Note that the stencil itself is delicate—i.e., there are lots of curving lines and little "bridges" that connect the parts of the design. Especially for big projects like a large room, have masking tape on hand to repair those bridges along the way.

The background here has been "cheeseclothed," a technique named for the gauzelike material with which glaze is applied. Cheeseclothing is from the "ragging" family of techniques. A range of techniques from that group would work well here, although cheeseclothing is partic-

ularly recommended because of the soft, subtle finish it creates. For a detailed guide to cheeseclothing and related techniques, see the *Cloth Distressing* chapter in the first volume of *Recipes for Surfaces*, page 107.

You can buy packages of cheesecloth in paint or hardware stores, home centers, and sometimes supermarkets (it is used in cooking to strain food). About three packages will be enough for a medium-size wall. Before you begin, run the cheesecloth through a washer (gentle cycle) and dryer to give it a softer texture.

The trickiest part of this project is cutting out the three stencils that make up the design. You'll find the patterns on pages 181-182.

1. Apply masking tape over edge of crown molding to keep any paint from getting on it. Pour paint into paint tray.

2. Bunch square of cheesecloth in your hand, tucking in edges to keep threads from getting in paint. Dip in paint, test on paper, then touch cloth to wall repeatedly, turning your wrist and arm so that different parts of the cloth touch the surface and thus create a variety of impressions. When cloth is almost dry, dip in paint again. Repeat process, working in 3-foot sections. Stand back from surface often to see overall effect. Apply paint lightly and build up slowly for even finish; avoid creating strong dark or light areas, which will pull the eye away from stenciling.

Follow the directions for transferring and cutting out a stencil on page 165, and see page 164 for additional guidelines. Cutting out these patterns is particularly challenging because of all the curves. Two tips: If you make a mistake, mend it with masking tape. And when cutting a curve, you may find it easier to move your stencil instead of your knife. Be sure to cut out the bow-tie-shaped registration marks on the side and bottom of each stencil; lining up the three stencils precisely is key to a professional look, and matching up the marks each time lets you do this.

Once cut, number your stencils and mark on each one (with a laundry marker) the words "front," "up," and "right" so that you can line them up correctly each time. It's easy to get mixed up in the heat of the project.

3

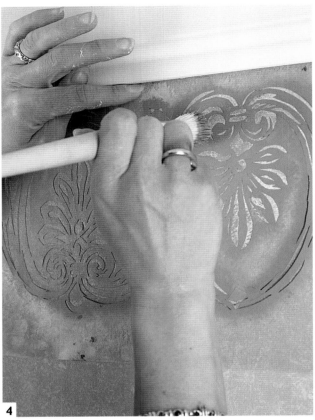

4

5

6

3. **Wearing mask and gloves, spray back of first stencil with adhesive. Align first stencil with edge of molding or ceiling line. Place small pieces of masking tape under each bow-tie shaped registration mark (this prevents paint not part of the pattern from getting on surface). Put some of first paint color on palette. Dip in 1-inch stenciling brush and dab off excess paint on paper (brush should be almost dry). Dab brush over registration marks first. Then fill in rest of pattern by patting brush firmly over stencil. Remove stencil carefully so that it doesn't rip. (Don't wipe stencils after use; they might rip. Just store flat.) Paint dries quickly; so you don't have to wait before going to next step.**

4. **Put second paint color on palette. Spray back of second stencil with adhesive. Using registration marks, align second stencil exactly over first. Dip second brush in paint, test on paper, then pat firmly—first over registration marks, then rest of stencil. Remove stencil carefully.**

5. **Repeat process, using third paint color, stenciling brush, and stencil, to complete one design.**

6. **Put first stencil up next to design you just completed, overlapping it slightly. (Re-spray stencil with adhesive, if needed.) Repeat steps 4 through 7 as many times as necessary to complete your project.**

7. **The subtle colors of the finished effect help convey a sense of depth.**

7

Tile

STENCILS

Grape-Leaf Motif

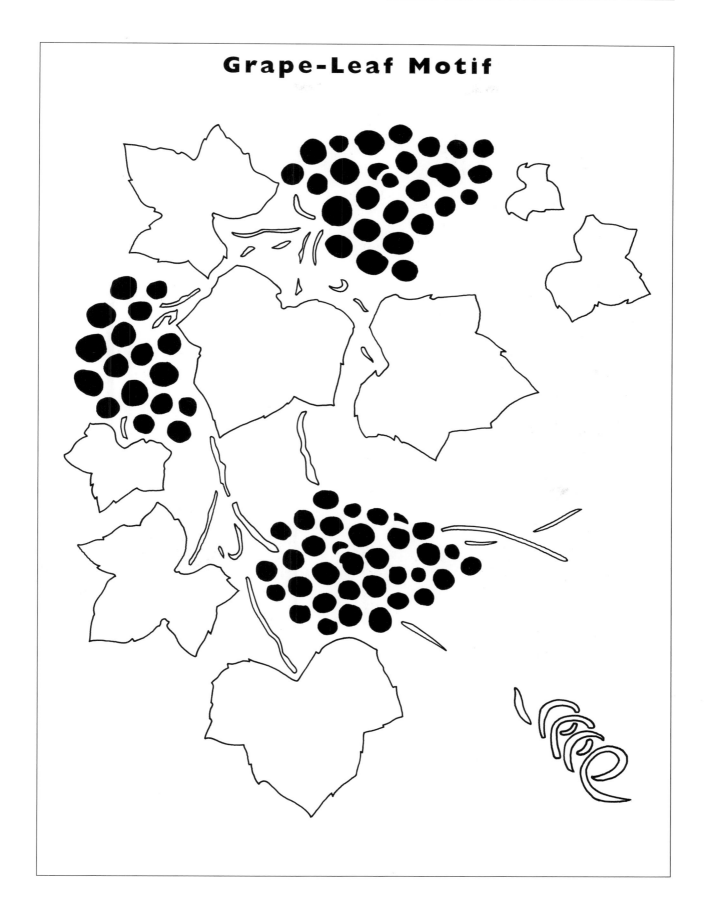

Leopard skin

STENCILS

Architectural Molding

Architectural Molding

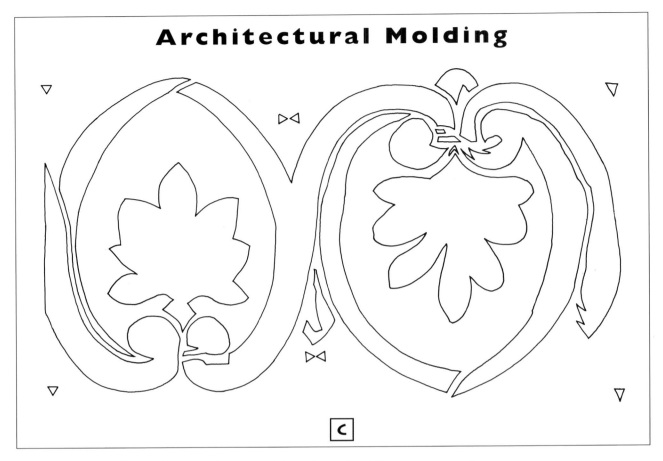

C

Recipe Paint Formulas

The following formulas were created using Benjamin Moore & Co. paint products, but they have been converted to generic terms (see chart below), so that other paint systems may be used. Please note if other systems are used, the colors may very slightly, and adjustments might need to be made. The easiest method to reproduce the colors is to take the following formulas to your local paint store, and have someone there mix the paint for you. The quantities of tints used in the formulas are for 32 parts increments per ounce. If your paint store uses 48 parts per ounce, they will have to modify the formulas accordingly.

Universal tint colors:

OY=Yellow ochre
RO=Red oxide/Venitian red
BK=Black/Lamp black
BB=Thalo blue
TG=Thalo green/Dark green
OG=Orange
CR=Red/Red-orange
MG=Magenta/Violet
GY=Lt. Gray toner/Raw umber
WH=White

Generic paint terms translated into Benjamin Moore & Co. brand names:

Latex flat=RWS
Latex eggshell=AquaVelvet
Latex semi-gloss=Aquaglo
Oil flat=Saniflat 204
Oil-based low luster=Dulamel eggshell 305
Oil-based semi-gloss=Satin Impervo
High-gloss oil base=Impervo
1 base=white or pastel base
2 base=Lt. pastel base
3 base=Medium or midtone base
4 base=Deeptone base
5 base=Ultradeep or neutral base

Copper Verdigris p.78
Base coat: Metallic copper spray paint or copper hobby paint in 2 oz. jars. *Applied finish:* 2 flat oil-based paints, Seafoam blue: 1 qt. 204-4A (4-BASE)/BK 5/BB-15/TG-20/WH-1; Seafoam green: 1 qt. 204-4A (4-BASE)/YE-4/BK-3/TG-18/WH-1 oz.

Bronze Verdigris p.80
Base coat: Oil-based semi-gloss bronze. *Applied finish:* 3 oil-based enamel paints, Verdigris green: 1 qt. 319-1A(1-BASE)/OY5/BB6/TG-5 1/2/GY-7; Sage green: 1 qt. 319-3A(3-BASE)/YE-6/BK-5 1/2/TG-28/WH-2; Pine green: 1 qt. 319-4A(4-BASE)/OY-5/BK-5/BB-5/TG-26/WH-16.

Rusted Metal p.82
Base coat: Walnut brown oil-based enamel, 235-5A(5-BASE)/OY-23/BK-19/CR-23. *Applied finish:* 3 oil-based enamel paints, Rust: 1 qt. eggshell oil 235-5A(5-BASE)/RO-16/BK-4/MG-20/WH-12; Ebony brown: 1 qt. eggshell oil 235-5A(5-BASE)/OY-14 1/2/RO-17/BB-25/WH-9; Honey: 1 qt. eggshell oil 235-5A(5-BASE)/OY-1 oz. 8/RO-3/BK-2/GY-1 oz. 8/WH-4; Liquid gold leaf (spray or brush).

Flagstone p.87
Base coat: Maize latex porch and floor paint, 1 qt. eggshell 319-3A/OY-11/BK-2 1/2/OG-2. *Applied finish:* 3 latex porch and floor paints, thinned with water; plus charcoal glazing liquid for final paint coat, Birch: 1 qt. eggshell 319-2A/OY-3 1/2/BK-7/TG-1 1/2; Charcoal: 1 qt. eggshell 319-5A/OY-24 1/2/BB-26 1/2/CR-28; Aubergine: 1 qt. eggshell 319-4A/RO-8/MG-11/BB-8/WH-16; Charcoal glaze 1 qt. oil-based semi-gloss 235-5A/OY-24 1/2/BB-26 1/2/CR-28. *Varnish:* Several coats required for floors.

Fieldstone p.90
Base coat: Dove white latex flat interior house paint (floor, porch, & deck paint), 1 qt. RWS 215-1A/OY-1/2. *Applied finish:* 2 oil-based enamel paints, Straw: 1 qt. RWS 215-4A/OY-30/OG-2 1/2/GY-16/WH-1 oz.; Ash: 1 qt. RWS 215-4A/OY-1 oz./RO-2/BK-27. *Varnish:* Required for floors.

Granite p.92
Base coat: Dove white latex semi-gloss interior house paint, 1 qt. 215-1A/OY-1/2. *Applied finish:* 4 latex eggshell interior house paint, Taupe: 1 qt. eggshell 319-4A(4-BASE)/OY-18/BK-14/MG-4/WH-22; Chalk: 1 qt. eggshell 319-1A(1-BASE)/OY -5/BK-3 1/2/GY-8/OG-2; Tawny: 1 qt. eggshell 319-3A (3-BASE)/OY-12/RO-2 1/2/ GY-8; Midnight gray: 1 qt. eggshell 319-5A(5-BASE) /OY-6/BK-2 oz. 4/MG-2. *Varnish:* Use water-based varnish.

Malachite p.96
Base coat: Clover latex semi-gloss interior house paint, 1 qt. latex interior semi-gloss 333-4A(4-BASE)/YE-4/TG-1 oz. 6/OG-2. *Glaze:* Oil-based glazing liquid and spruce alkyd low-luster paint, 1 qt. oil-based semi-gloss 235-5A(5-BASE)/YE-6/OY-10/BK-26/TG-4 oz. 24. *Varnish:* Use water-based varnish.

Red Marble p.103
Base coat: Melon latex semi-gloss interior house paint 1 qt. latex semi-gloss interior 333-4A(4-BASE)/OY-4/OG-1 oz. 24/GY-28/WH-8. *Glazes:* Gold leaf oil-based enamel paint, plus oil-based glazing liquid and 3 alkyd low-luster enamel paints, Tomato: 1 qt. oil-based semi-gloss 235-5A/RO-2/BK-1/2/CR-1 oz. 28; Raspberry: 1 qt. oil-based semi-gloss 235-5A(5-BASE)/MG-5/CR-2 oz. /GY-28; Plum: 1 qt. oil-based semi-gloss 235-5A(5-BASE)/OY-9/BK-16/MG-1 oz. 12. *Varnish:* Use water-based varnish.

Blue Marble p.106
Base coat: Powder blue latex semi-gloss interior paint, 1 qt. RWS 215-2A/BK 1/2/BB5 1/2/MG-1/2GY-12. *Applied finish:* 4 latex interior paint colors, plus silver foil for veining, Sail blue: 1 qt. RWS 215-4A/YE-3 1/2/BK-2/MG-19/WH-18/BB-29; Caribbean green: 1 qt. RWS 319-4A(4-BASE)/OY-22/BB-24/TG-6; Dark teal: 1 qt. RWS 215-5A(5-BASE)/BK-11/BB-1 oz. 8/TG-24/WH-2; Salmon: 1 qt. RWS 215-4A/OG-1 oz. 11/CR-4/GY-2. *Varnish:* Use water-based varnish.

Sedimentary-Style Marble p.110
Base coat: Dove white latex semi-gloss interior house paint, 1 qt. RWS 215-1A/OY-1/2. *Glazes:* Oil-based glazing liquid and 5 alkyd low-luster paints, Buff: 1 qt. oil-based semi-gloss 235-2A/OY-13/RO-4/GY-1 oz.; Saddle: 1 qt. oil-based semi-gloss 235-4A/OY-26/RO-18/BB-3 1/2/OG-12/WH-28; Turquoise: 1 qt. oil-based semi-gloss 235-4A/OY-3 1/2/BB-10/TG-30/WH-16; Eggplant: 1 qt. oil-based semi-gloss 235-5A/RO-9/BK-1/BB-11/MG-11/WH-16; Clay: 1 qt. oil-based semi-gloss 235-5A/DY-4/RO-16/BB-3/CR-1 oz. 6. *Varnish:* Use water-based varnish.

Fresco p.117
Base coat: Linen white latex semi-gloss interior house paint, 1 qt. latex interior semi-gloss 333-70/1 qt. 333-1A/OY-2/OG-1/2/GY-2. *Glaze:* Oil-based glazing liquid and pumpkin alkyd low-luster paint, 1 qt. oil-based semi-gloss 235-5A/OY-12/OG-30/GY-10/WH-8. *Varnish:* Optional.

Leather p.119
Base coat: Barn red latex semi-gloss interior house paint, 1 qt. latex interior semi-gloss 333-5A/RO-1/BK-2 1/2/MG-7/CR-2 oz. 6. *Glaze:* Oil-based glazing liquid and garnet alkyd low-luster paint, 1 qt. oil-based semi-gloss 235-5A/RO-1/BK-2 1/2/MG-1 oz. 8/OG-1 oz. *Varnish:* Optional.

Stucco p.121 *Base coat:* Dove white latex flat interior house paint, 1 qt. RWS 215-1A/OY-1/2. *Glazes:* Watered-down latex paint (20% paint, 80% water); Light maize: 1 qt. RWS 215-2A/YE-29/OY-3/OG-6/GY-22; Light ash: 1 qt. RWS-4A (4-BASE)/OY-18 1/2/BK-16/OG-7/WH-1 oz. *Varnish:* No (sheen would detract from look).

Cloudy Sky p.124
Base coat: Sky blue latex flat interior house paint, 1 qt. RWS 215-1A/BK-2/BB-6 1/2/MG-1. *Applied finish:* White oil-based enamel paint, 1 qt. oil-based semi-gloss. *Varnish:* No.

Brick p.126
Base coat: 2 latex semi-gloss interior house paints, Mortar: 1 qt. RWS 215-4A/OY-12 1/2/BB-6/OG-30/2H-10; Melon: 1 qt. latex semi-gloss interior 333-4A/OY-16/RO-2/BB-1/MG-2/OG-1 oz. 16/GY-4/WH-14. *Applied finish:* 3 oil-based enamel paints, Terra cotta: 1 qt. oil-based semi-gloss 235-5A/RO-25/BB-1/MG-1/WH-24; Brown: 1 qt. oil-based semi-gloss 235-5A/OY-1 oz. 12/RO-6 1/2/BK-14 1/2/OG-6/WH-6; Black: Oil-based enamel paint. *Varnish:* Required for floors.

Moire p.130
Base coat: Light blue latex interior paint, 1 qt. RWS 215-1A/BK-1/BB-8/CR-3. *Glaze:* Oil-based glazing liquid and sapphire alkyd low-luster paint, 1 qt. oil-based semi-gloss 235-5A(5-BASE) /BB-1 oz. /MG-3 oz./BK-2. *Varnish:* Optional.

Feather-Duster Finish p.137
Base coat: Coral latex semi-gloss interior house paint, 1 qt. RWS 215-2A/OG-24/CR-12. *Applied finish:* Salmon latex semi-gloss interior house paint, 1 qt. RWS 215-3A/YE-5/OG-22/CR-24. *Varnish:* Optional.

Corduroy Ragging On p.139
Base coat: Plum latex semi-gloss interior house paint, 1 qt. RWS 215-5A(5-BASE)/BK-9/MG-2 oz. 24. *Glaze:* Oil-based glazing liquid and rose oil-based enamel paint, 1 qt. oil-based semi-gloss 215-1A/OY-1/MG-9 1/2/BB-1/OG-8. *Varnish:* Optional.

Corduroy Ragging Off p.141
Base coat: Bone latex semi-gloss interior house paint, 1 qt. latex interior semi-gloss 333-1A/2-OY-10/BK-3/CR-2/GY-6. *Glaze:* Oil-based glazing liquid and putty alkyd low-luster enamel paint, 1 qt. oil-based semi-gloss 235-5A(5-BASE)/OY-1 oz. 4/BB-5/MG-10/WH-1 oz. 4. *Varnish:* Optional.

Plastic-Wrap Ragging Off p.144
Base coat: Dove white latex semi-gloss interior house paint, 1 qt. RWS 215-1A/OY-1/2. *Glaze:* Oil-based glazing liquid and rose alkyd low-luster enamel paint, 1 qt. oil-based semi-gloss 215-1A/OY-1/MG-9 1/2/BB-1/OG-8. *Varnish:* Optional.

Plastic Bag Ragging Off p.146
Base coat: Robin's egg blue latex semi-gloss interior house paint, 1 qt. RWS 215-1A/BK-1/BB-6/TG-16/GY-6. *Glaze:* Oil-based glazing liquid and moss green paint, 1 qt. oil-based semi-gloss 215-4A/OY-29/TG-11/BK-14/WH-14. *Varnish:* Optional.

Spattering In Four Colors p.148
Base coat: Butter latex semi-gloss interior house paint, 1 qt. RWS 215-1A/YE-5 1/2/OY-1 1/2/OG-2 drops/ GY-1. *Applied finish:* 4 latex semi-gloss interior house paints, Teal: 1 qt. RWS 215-4A/BK-4/BB-24/TG-24/GY-1 oz.; Robin's egg blue: 1 qt. RWS 215-1A/BK-1/BB-6/TG16/GY-6; Dusty rose: 1 qt. RWS 215-2A/OG-20/CR-16/YE-4; Sunflower: RWS color #319/1 qt. RWS 215-2A/YE-1 oz. 12/OG-1/2/CR-1/2. *Varnish:* Optional.

Blue Spatter Finish p.150
Base coat: White linen latex semi-gloss interior house paint, 1 qt. RWS 215-1A 2/OY-2/OG-1/4/GY-2. *Applied finish:* 4 latex flat paints, Sail blue: 1 qt. RWS 215-4A/YE-3 1/2/BB-29/BK-2/WH-18/MG-19; Cornflower: 1 qt. RWS 215-2A/BK-4/BB-16/MG-5/CR-1/GY-6; Navy: 1 qt. RWS 215-5A/BB-1 oz. 24/BK-11/CR-16/MG-6/WH-19; Delft blue: 1 qt. RWS 215-1A/BK-1/BB-4/CR-1/2/MG-2/GY-2. *Varnish:* Optional.

Flogging p.151
Base coat: White linen latex semi-gloss interior house paint, 1 qt. latex interior semi-gloss 333-70/1 qt. 333-1A/OY-2/OG-1/2/GY-2. *Glazes:* Oil-based glazing liquid and 2 alkyd low-luster paints, Mustard: 1 qt. oil-based semi-gloss 235-4A(4-BASE)/YE-1 oz. 3/OG-5 1/2/GY-17/WH-28; Brown: 1 qt. oil-based semi-gloss 235-4A(4-BASE)/OY-2 oz. 4/RO-13/BK-16. *Varnish:* Optional.

Crackle Glaze p.157
Base coat: Palamino brown oil-based eggshell paint, 1 qt. 305-4A/OY-3 oz. 16/RO-6/BK-4. *Applied finish:* Layer of latex-based crackle glaze (see *Sources*), then layer of hazelnut latex paint, 1 qt. eggshell 319-3A/RO-1 1/2/BK-3/OG-2/GY-6. *Varnish:* Use water-based varnish.

Decoupage p.160
Base coat: Almond spray paint. *Glaze:* Oil-based glazing liquid and white oil-based enamel paint. *Lining:* Dark green oil-based enamel paint, 1 qt. 235-5A (5-BASE)/ OY-26/RO-4/BK-1 oz. 28/TG-1 oz. 8. *Varnish:* Use water-based varnish.

Tile p.166
Base coat: Celery latex semi-gloss interior house paint, 1 qt. RWS 319-2A(2-BASE)/OY-14/TG-5 1/2/BK-6/GY-4/WH-12. *Applied finish:* Tan latex semi-gloss interior house paint, 1 qt. RWS 319-3A(3-BASE) /OY-21/RO-1/BK-3. *Varnish:* Use water-based varnish.

Grape-Leaf Motif p.168
Base coat: Dove white latex flat interior house paint, 1 qt. RWS 215-1A/OY-1/2. *Glazes:* For ragged background--50% flat latex interior house paint and 50% water, Pearl: 1 qt. RWS 215-1A/OY-2/BB-1/2/MG-1, Sky blue: 1 qt. RWS 215-1A/BK-2/BB-6 1/2/MG-1. *Stencil paints:* Acrylic stencil paints (5 grape colors), Royal Violet: 1 qt. RWS 215-5A/BB-22/MG-1 oz. 16/CR-12; Heather: 1 qt. RWS 215-3A/YE-3 1/2/BB-6/MG-1 oz. 8; Lavender: 1 qt. RWS 215-4A/BK-1/BB-3/MG-28; Blue Ink: 1 qt. RWS 215-5A/BK-18/BB-1 oz. 18/CR-8; Tapestry wine: 1 qt. RWS 215-5A/BK-6/MG-17/CR-2 oz. 20. (continued next column)

4 shades of green: Basil: 1 qt. RWS 215-3A/OY-23/BK-3/TG-3; Indian: 1 qt. RWS 215-5A/YE-1 oz. 16/BB-10 1/2/OG-9/WH-13; Hunter: 1 qt. RWS 215-5A/OY-11/BK-18/TG-1 oz. 20; Thicket: 1 qt. RWS 215-5A/OY-1 oz. 13/BK-28/TG-20. *Varnish:* Optional.

Leopard skin p.172
Base coat: White linen latex semi-gloss interior house paint, 1 qt. latex interior semi-gloss 333-1A/OY-2/OG-1/2/GY-2. *Glazes:* Oil-based glazing liquid and 2 alkyd low-luster paints, Mustard: 1 qt. oil-based semi-gloss 235-4A(4-BASE)/YE-1 oz. 3/OG-5 1/2/GY-17/WH-28; Brown: 1 qt. oil-based semi-gloss 235-4A(4-BASE)/OY-2 oz. 4/RO-13/BK-16. *Stenciling:* Chocolate: 1 qt. oil-based semi-gloss 235-5A(5-BASE)/OY-18/RO-14/BK-1 oz. 14. *Varnish:* Optional.

Architectural Molding p.174
Base coat: Coffee latex flat interior house paint, 1 qt. RWS 215-2A(2-BASE)/OY-22/RO-4/BK-5/GY-6. *Applied finish:* 4 latex flat interior house paints, Pearl: 1 qt. RWS 215-1A/OY-2/BB-1/2/MG-1; Latte: 1 qt. RWS 215-1A/OY-8/RO-1/BK-1 1/2/GY-8; Cappuccino: 1 qt. RWS 215-4A(4-BASE)/OY-6/BK-5/OG-14/GY-24/WH-8; Espresso: 1 qt. RWS 215-4A(4-BASE)/OY-3/BB-10/OG-28/WH-8. *Varnish:* Optional.

SOURCES

SUPPLIES AND TOOLS

Some of the paints, tools, and materials for the finishes in this book were provided by:

HOME DEPOT
2727 Paces Ferry Rd.
Atlanta, GA 30339
Retail stores nationwide offering a wide range of paints, brushes, tools, safety equipment, and more. For store locations in your area, call the Home Depot District Office nearest you:
California-
(714) 738-5200;
Canada-
(416) 609-0582;
Florida-
(813) 289-0040;
Illinois-
(708) 413-4900;
New Jersey-
(908) 752-1700.

PEARL ART & CRAFT AND PEARL PAINT STORES
House and artists' paints, brushes, sponges, graining tools, stenciling materials, safety equipment; general art supplies.

Store locations:
New York City-
(212) 431-7932;
East Meadow, NY-
(516) 731-3700;
Paramus, NJ-
(201) 447-0300;
Woodbridge, NJ-
(908) 634-9400;
Cherry Hill, NJ-
(609) 667-6500;
Fort Lauderdale, FL-
(305) 564-5700;
Miami, FL-
(305) 251-5700;
North Miami, FL-
(305) 651-9600;
Altamonte Springs, FL-
(407) 831-3000;
Tampa, FL-
(813) 286-8000;
Alexandria, VA-
(703) 960-3900;
Cambridge, MA-
(617) 547-6600;
Rockville, MD-
(301) 816-2900;
Atlanta, GA-
(404) 233-9400;
Houston, TX-
(713) 977-5600.

Mail order available through
**Pearl Paint,
308 Canal St.,
New York, NY 10013;
call (212) 221-6845.**

OTHER SOURCES INCLUDE:

AIR NOUVEAU
1985 Swathmore Ave.,
Lakewood, NJ 08701;
(908) 364-2111
The Air Nouveau Stencil Burner, an electric tool for cutting out stencils, is available through mail order from the company.

ALBERT CONSTANTINE & SON
2050 Eastchester Rd.
Bronx, NY 10461
(800) 223-8087
Retail store and mail order. Paint strippers, brushes, varnishes.

ART ESSENTIAL OF NEW YORK
3 Cross St.
Suffern, NY 10901-4601
(914) 368-1100
Distributor of gold leaf supplies. Call for nearest retail store carrying these products.

Art Supply Warehouse
360 Main Ave. (Rte. 7)
Norwalk, CT 06851
(203) 849-1112
(800) 243-5038 for mail order; or, (203) 846-2270 for mail order in Connecticut. Mail order and retail artists' paints, brushes, general art supplies.

BINNEY AND SMITH
1100 Church Lane
P.O. Box 431
Easton, PA 18044-0431
(800) 272-9652; or,
(215) 253-6271 in PA
Publishers of Liquitex ® Color Maps and Mixing Guides. Call for nearest retail store carrying products.

CHROMATIC PAINT CORP.
5555 Spaulding Dr.
Norcross, GA 30092
(914) 947-3210
Manufacturer of japan colors. Call for nearest retail store carrying products.

DICK BLICK FINE ART CO.
P.O. Box 1267
Galesburg, IL 61401
(309) 343-6181
(800) 447-8192
for mail order.
Retail stores in Midwest and mail order. Artists' paints, brushes, general art supplies.

DOVER PUBLICATIONS
Dept. 23
31 E. 2nd St.
Mineola, NY 11501
Write for free crafts and fine-arts catalog and for Dover Pictorial Archive Series.

EAGLE SUPPLY CO.
327 W. 42nd St.
New York, NY 10036
(212) 246-6180
Sign painters' supplies. Will do mail order via UPS C.O.D.

FINESSE PINSTRIPING
P.O. Box 1428, Linden
Hill Station
Flushing, NY 11354
(800) 228-1258; or (800)
696-5699 in NY
Manufacturer of pinstriping
tape. Call for nearest distributor of the products.

FROG TOOL CO.
700 W. Jackson Blvd.
Chicago, IL 60606
(312) 648-1270
Mail order and retail paint
strippers, brushes, varnishes.

GRAND CENTRAL ARTISTS' MATERIALS
14 E. 41st St.
New York, NY 10017
(212) 679-0023
Retail and mail order
general art and graphic arts
supplies.

GAIL GRISI STENCILING
405 Haddon Ave.
Haddonfield, NJ 08033
(800) 338-1325; or, in NJ,
(609) 354-1757
Retail stores in NJ and mail
order. Precut stencils and
paints.

LAB SAFETY SUPPLY
P.O. Box 1368
Janesville, WI
53547-1368
(800) 356-0783
Manufacturer and
distributor of safety clothing
and equipment; catalog
available.

LAURA ASHLEY,
6 St. James Ave.
Boston, MA 02116
(800) 367-2000
Limited selection of stencils,
stencil paints, and stencil
brushes. Laura Ashley
Home mail-order catalog
and Laura Ashley retail
stores nationwide; call for
shop nearest you.

Lee Valley Tools
1080 Morrison Dr.
Ottawa, Ontario K2H
8K7 Canada
(613) 596-0350 in US and
613 area code
(800) 267-8767 in southeastern Canada
(800) 267-8757 in western
and northern Canada
Brushes, paints, glazes. Mail
order available.

LEE'S ART SHOP
220 W. 57th St.
New York, NY 10019
(212) 247-0110
Retail and mail order.
General art supplies,
including sea sponges and
color-mixing charts.

LEO UHLFELDER CO.
420 S. Fulton Ave.
Mount Vernon, NY
10553
(914) 664-8701
Importer and manufacturer
of gold leaf and brushes.
Call for nearest retailer carrying the products.

LIBERTY PAINTS
Rtes. 66 and 23B
Hudson, NY 12534
(518) 828-4060
Retail and mail order. Wide
range of products including
paints, glazes, and brushes.

NEW YORK CENTRAL ART SUPPLY
62 Third Ave.
New York, NY 10003
(212) 473-7705 for store
(800) 950-6111 for mail
order; or, in NY
(212) 477-0400
Retail and mail order for
general art supplies.

POTTERY BARN
100 North Point St.
San Francisco, CA
94133
(415) 421-7900
(800) 922-5507 for mail
order. Mail order, plus
retails stores in 15 states;
call for nearest location.
Metallic paints, marbling kits.

RENOVATOR'S SUPPLY
Renovator's Old Mill
Millers Falls, MA 10349
(413) 659-2241
Company offers catalog that
includes paints in traditional
colors.

SAM FLAX INC.
39 W. 19th St.
New York, NY 10011
(212) 620-3010
(800) 628-9512 for mail
order. Retail stores nationwide and mail order.
General art and graphic arts
supplies.

SEPP LEAF PRODUCTS
381 Park Ave. So.,
Ste. 1301
New York, NY 10016
(212) 683-2840
Mail order gold-leaf supplies.

T.J. RONAN PAINT CORP.
749 E. 135th St.
Bronx, NY 10454
(800) 24-RONAN; or, in
NY, (212) 292-1100
Manufacturer of japan colors; call for nearest store
carrying the products.

3M CORP.
3M Center
St. Paul, MN 55144
(800) 364-3577
Manufacturer of low-tack
masking tapes, heavy-duty
stripping pad used in
"Spattering" technique, and
more; call for product information and nearest store
carrying the products.

UTRECT MANUFACTURING CORP.
33 35th St.
Brooklyn, NY 11232
(718) 768-2525
(800) 223-9132 for mail
order. General art supplies
via mail order and retail
stores in several states; call
for locations.

WINDSOR & NEWTON
11 Constitution Ave.
Piscataway, NJ 08855
(908) 562-0770
Distributor of artists' paints
and brushes. Call for nearest
retailer carrying the products.

WOOD FINISHING SUPPLY CO.
100 Throop St.
Palmyra, NY 14522
(315) 597-3743
Mail order glazes, japan
colors, graining combs, gold
leaf, brushes, varnishes, and
other supplies.

WOODCRAFTERS LUMBER SALES
212 Northeast Sixth Ave.
Portland, OR 97232
(800) 777-3709
Retail and mail order paint
strippers, varnishes, brushes, and specialty moldings
and architectural elements.

THE WOODWORKER'S STORE
21801 Industrial Blvd.
Rogers, MN 55374
(612) 428-2199
Paint strippers, brushes,
varnishes, wood fillers. Mail
order and retail stores; call
for locations.

WOODWORKER'S SUPPLY OF NEW MEXICO
5604 Alameda Place NE
Albuquerque, NM 87113
(800) 645-9292; or, in
NM, (505) 821-0500
Mail order. Paint strippers,
glazes, varnishes, graining
tools and other supplies.

HOUSE PAINT, GLAZE, AND VARNISH MANUFACTURERS

ABSOLUTE COATINGS
34 Industrial St.
Bronx, NY 10461
(800) 221-8010; in New
York, (212) 892-1800
Varnishes available
nationwide.

BENJAMIN MOORE & CO.
51 Chestnut Ridge Rd.
Montvale, NJ 07645
(800) 344-0400
Products available nationwide through dealers.

FULLER-O'BRIEN CORP.
450 E. Grand Ave.
South San Francisco,
CA 94080
(800) 368-2068 in the east
(800) 338-8084 in the west
Products available nationwide through Fuller-O'Brien
stores and dealers.

LONG ISLAND PAINT CO.
P.O. Box 189
Glen Cove, NY 11542
(516) 676-6600
House and casein paints by
mail or through retail stores
in NY and RI.

MCCLOSKEY VARNISH CO.
7600 State Rd.
Philadelphia, PA 19136
(800) 345-4530
Ready-mixed glazes, flatting
oil, and varnishes available
through dealers.

MARTIN-SENOUR PAINTS
101 Prospect Ave.
Cleveland, OH 44115
(800) 542-8468
Products available nationwide through dealers.

PRATT & LAMBERT
P.O. Box 22
Buffalo, NY 14240
(716) 873-6000
(800) 289-7728
Paints, ready-mixed glazes,
and varnishes available
nationwide.

SAMUEL CABOT INC.
100 Hale St.
Newburyport, MA
01950
(800) 877-8246
(508) 465-1900
Products available
nationwide.

SHERWIN WILLIAMS
101 Prospect Ave.
Cleveland, OH 44115
(800) 752-8468
Products available nationwide through Sherwin
Williams stores.

FOR FURTHER READING

Classic Paints and Faux Finishes: How to Use Natural Materials and Authentic Techniques in Today's Decorating by Annie Sloan and Kate Gwynn; Reader's Digest, Pleasantville, NY; 1993.

The Complete Book of Decorative Painting Techniques by Annie Sloan and Kate Gwynn; Salem House Publishers, Topsfield, MA; 1988.

The Country Diary Book of Stenciling by Rowena Stott and Jane Cheshire; Viking, New York; 1988.

Decorating with Paint by Jocasta Innes; Harmony Books, New York; 1986.

Designer's Guide to Surfaces and Finishes by Penny Radford; Whitney Library of Design, New York; 1984.

Floorworks by Akiko Busch; Bantam Books, New York; 1988.

The New Paint Magic by Jocasta Innes; Pantheon Books, New York; 1992.

Parry's Graining and Marbling by Brian Rhodes and John Windsor; BSP Professional Books, Boston; 1985.

Professional Painted Finishes: A Guide to the Art and Business of Decorative Painting by Inna Brosseau Marx, Allen Marx, and Robert Marx; Whitney Library of Design, New York; 1991.

Recipes for Surfaces by Mindy Drucker and Pierre Finkelstein; Fireside Books; New York; 1993.

COLOR GUIDES

Color Harmony: A Guide to Creative Color Combinations by Chijiiwa Hideake; Rockport Publishers, Rockport, MA; 1987.

Color Image Scale by Shigenobu Kobayashi; Kodansha International, New York; 1991.

Color in Decoration by Annie Sloan and Kate Gwynn; Little, Brown & Co., New York; 1990.

Color: Natural Palettes for Painted Rooms by Donald Kaufman and Taffy Dahl; Clarkson N. Potter/Publishers, New York; 1992.

index